HARVEY'S LANGUAGE COURSE

ELEMENTARY GRAMMAR

AND

COMPOSITION

BY

THOS. W. HARVEY, A. M.

Originally published by
Van Antwerp, Bragg & Co.

This edition published by

MOTT
MEDIA

This edition © 1986 by Mott Media, Inc.
1000 East Huron Street, Milford, Michigan 48042

ISBN 0-88062-041-2

PRESENT PUBLISHER'S PREFACE

Thomas W. Harvey's *Elementary Grammar and Composition* was published by the same company which produced the McGuffey *Readers*. It had great appeal in its time, having particularly big sales in the midwest. This text is intended to precede Harvey's complete and classic *English Grammar* book, and students may begin to use it in middle grades of elementary school—from about grades four to six.

In updating this textbook, we revised the punctuation section and punctuation usage throughout the book to conform to contemporary usage. In grammar, a few rules were dropped and a few added, but grammatical rules change slowly over time, so not much of this revising was necessary. Usage changes somewhat more rapidly, so we had some updatings in verb forms, phraseology, hyphenations, and forms of friendly and business letters. Many of Harvey's examples are from the Bible and other literature, so they are left as they were, but some of the everyday examples are updated. A sentence about a horse and buggy, for instance, may be rewritten to one about a car.

All revisions conform to the authority of *Webster's New International Dictionary, Second Edition*. Other standard references were consulted as needed during the work. Several comments from *The Elements of Style* by Strunk and White have been quoted herein to bring insight to difficult language problems. For the masterful job of updating this textbook, credit belongs to Eric C. Wiggin.

Through all the revisions, we have left the content as close to the original as possible. The famous Harvey grammar is here for modern users. We proudly present this classic to young students and their teachers everywhere.

George M. Mott, President
MOTT MEDIA, INC.

PREFACE

This work is a revision of the author's Elementary Grammar, first published in 1869. Part I consists of lessons in technical grammar, sentence-making, and composition. Great care has been taken never to define a term or to enunciate a principle without first preparing the mind of the pupil to grasp and comprehend the meaning and use of the term defined or the principle enunciated. Ideas are first developed by intelligent questioning and appropriate illustrations then clothed in words.

Sentence making and composition are, it is believed, presented in a natural and attractive manner. Words are given for the pupil to use in sentences. At first, all the words are given, then a part of them. Having acquired some facility in the construction of sentences, the pupil is next taught to use groups of words, phrases, and clauses as single words.

In composition, the pupil is first taught to tell what he sees in a picture, then to answer questions concerning the objects represented in it. The description and the answers following it make a composition. He is next taught to study a picture and to exercise his inventive powers in writing short stories suggested by it.

This course of instruction is introductory to that given in Part II which contains a concise yet exhaustive statement of the properties and modifications of the different parts of speech, as well as carefully prepared models for parsing and analysis, rules of syntax, and plans for the description of single objects—a continuation of the composition work begun in Part I.

It has been said that there is no royal road to geometry. The same may be said of grammar and composition. The meaning and application of technical terms must be learned, sentences must be analyzed, and words must be parsed, before the student can comprehand the philosophy that underlies the correct use of any language. The labor necessary to secure facility and accuracy in the use of one's mother tongue may be made attractive, but it cannot be dispensed with; neither can it be materially lessened. All that is claimed for this work is that it shows how this labor should be expended to secure the best results.

Thomas Harvey

June 1880

CONTENTS

PART I

PART II

PART III

GRAMMAR

PART I

ELEMENTARY COURSE

1. OBJECTS

1. The **senses**—We have five senses: *seeing, hearing, feeling, tasting,* and *smelling.*

When we see, feel, taste, or smell things, or hear sounds, we are said to *perceive* them.

I drop a book upon the floor. A force called *gravitation* draws it toward the center of the earth. We cannot *perceive* this force, but we are *conscious of* it—that is, we know such a force must exist.

We are conscious of many other things that we cannot perceive; as, *love, hatred, joy, sorrow,* vexed.

All these things are called *objects.* What, then, is an *object*?

2. An **object** is anything we can perceive or of which we may be conscious.

When we think, we think of objects; when we talk, we talk about objects; when we write, we write about objects.

When we talk or write, we use *words* to express our thoughts. What, then, is a *word*?

3. A **word** is a syllable or a combination of syllables used in the expression of thought.

Questions—How many senses have we? Name them. Name some things that we can perceive. Name some things that we cannot perceive but of which we may be conscious. What is an object? What is a word?

2. DEFINITIONS

1. Language is the expression of thought by means of words.

When we talk, we express our ideas by spoken words. This is called *spoken language*.

2. Spoken language is the expression of ideas by the voice.

When we write or print our thoughts, we use letters which represent sounds. This is called *written language*.

3. Written language is the expression of thought by the use of written or printed characters.

4. Grammar treats of the principles and usages of language.

5. English grammar teaches how to speak and write the English language correctly.

Questions—What is language? Spoken language? Written language? Grammar? English grammar?

3. THE SENTENCE

What is the color of chalk? It is *white*. Chalk breaks easily: is it *tough* or *brittle*? It is *brittle*. We cannot see through it: hence we say it *opaque*.

We will join the words *white*, *brittle*, and *opaque* with the word *chalk*, thus:

> Chalk is white.
> Chalk is brittle.
> Chalk is opaque.

Each of these groups of words makes complete sense. Each is called a *sentence*.

1. A **sentence** is a group of words making complete sense.

Each group is also called a *proposition*.

2. A **proposition** is a thought expressed in words.

In writing sentences, observe the following directions:

1st. Begin each sentence with a capital letter.

2d. Spell each word correctly.

3d. Place a period [.] at the end of every sentence that declares something or makes a command.

4th. Place an interrogation point [?] at the end of every question. An interrogation point is also known as a question mark.

5th. Never divide a syllable at the end of a line.

Questions—What is a sentence? A proposition? Give the directions for writing sentences.

4. SENTENCE MAKING

I

When I say, "The window is open," I state a fact, using what is called a *declarative sentence*.

1. A **declarative sentence** is a sentence used in stating a fact.

When I say, "Is the window open?" I ask a question, using an *interrogative sentence*.

2. An **interrogative sentence** is a sentence used in asking a question.

Form declarative sentences out of the following words.

1. Iceland, very, is, in, it, cold. 2. Lesson, an, this, easy, is. 3. June, cherries, in, ripe, are. 4. Is, house, our, hill, the, on. 5. Always, good, happy, are, students. 6. Cap, river, into, the, fell, boy's, red, the, little. 7. Deep, our, is, street, very, in, snow, the. 8. Corn, spring, the, in, plants, farmer. 9. Ice, the, smooth, when, I, skate, to, like, very, is.

Form interrogative sentences out of the following words.

1. Lemons, where, grow, do. 2. Is, sick, today, brother, John's. 3. Cold, it, very, was, yesterday. 4. Aunt, does, the, tollgate, live, your, beyond, river, the, over. 5. Writing, exercise, isn't, pleasant, a. 6. You, school, at, not, yesterday, were. 7. Pick, white, I, this, may, rose.

Note—Write other groups and require the pupils to arrange them into sentences. Use this exercise until the pupils can easily and readily construct sentences containing not fewer than fifteen words.

Questions—What is a declarative sentence? An interrogative sentence? Repeat the directions to be observed in writing sentences.

II

When I say, "Clarence, open the window," I make a command; and when I say, "Please forgive me," I express an entreaty. In each instance I use an *imperative sentence.*

3. An **imperative sentence** is a sentence used in expressing a command or an entreaty.

When I say, "Oh, that window is open again!" I express some feeling or emotion, using an *exclamatory sentence.*

4. An **exlamatory sentence** is a sentence used in expressing some feeling or emotion.

An exclamation point (!) is usually placed after an exclamatory sentence.

Form imperative sentences out of the following words.

1. Go, your, seats, to, boys. 2. Home, go, once, at, Ponto. 3. Me, your, lend, book, Jane. 4. Minutes, lesson, ten, pupils, study, the. 5. Question, Susan, this, answer. 6. Skates, John, me, have, let, my. 7. Book, put, shelf, the, on, the. 8. Parents, obey, your, always. 9. Bicycle, into, the, wheel, the, Eddie, garage.

Form exclamatory sentences out of the following words.

1. Am, ha, ha, ha, I, it, of, glad. 2. Clock, four, listen, strikes, the. 3. Pretty, is, oh, she, how. 4. Don't, it, ugh, like, I. 5. Alone, hey, me, let.

Tell the kinds of sentences in the following exercises.

1. The winds bring perfume. 2. Where is my new book? 3. Go to the ant thou sluggard! 4. Scram—go away! 5. Necessity is the mother of invention. 6. Does God uniformly work in one way? 7. Oh, how I trembled with disgust! 8. Be not forward in the presence of your superiors. 9. Lend me your wings! I mount! I fly!

Tell the kinds of sentences in your reading lessons. Change the form of these sentences from declarative to interrogative, etc.

Questions—What is an imperative sentence? An exclamatory sentence? What mark is usually placed after an exclamatory sentence?

5. QUOTATION MARKS

The man yawned, and said, "How sleepy I am!"

In this sentence, these marks (") are placed before the exact words that the man spoke, and these (") after them. They are called *quotation marks*.

Quotation marks should be used when we quote the exact language of another.

Such a quotation should begin with a capital letter.

When we state what another says without using his *exact language* quotation marks should not be used. In this book, the answers supposed to be given by the pupils to the questions asked by the teacher are usually not quoted.

Use quotation marks and capital letters properly in these sentences.

1. Did your mother send you? asked the merchant, gruffly.
2. The general said, be ready to start at 5 a.m.
3. Will you come into my parlor? said the spider to the fly.
4. The pupils kept repeating, four times three are twelve, four times three are twelve, for at least three minutes.

Question—When should quotation marks be used?

6. PARTS OF SPEECH

"Scholars study." What word is here used instead of the names of the persons of whom we are speaking? "**Scholars.**" What word tells what scholars *do*? "**Study.**"

"Good scholars study." What word here describes scholars? "**Good.**"

"Good scholars study diligently." What word here tells *how* good scholars study? "**Diligently.**"

Words, then, not only have different meanings, but they are also used in different ways.

They can be divided into classes according to their meaning and use. These classes are called *parts of speech*.

Parts of speech are the classes into which words are divided according to their meaning and use.

It is necessary to know its meaning and use in order to determine to which class any word belongs.

Questions—What are parts of speech? What is necessary in order to determine the class to which any word belongs?

THE NOUN

7. ORAL LESSON

What are the words *boy*, *girl*, *city*, *door*, *window*, *book*, *desk*? They are names of objects.

That is correct. They are the *names* of objects, not the objects themselves. Because each word is a name, it is called a *noun*, which means a *name*.

1. A noun is a name; as, *boy*, *John*, *railroad*.

What are the words *house*, *farm*, *garden*, *dog*, *horse*, *blacksmith*, *merchant*? They are nouns. Why? Because they are names.

What are the words *Mary*, *John*, *Washington*, *Chicago*, *Ohio*, *America*? They are nouns. Why? Because they are names.

Can the name *boy* be applied to any boy in the school, or in the world? It can. It is a name, then, which is *common* to all boys; that is, it can be applied to each of them. So, also, the name *girl* is common to all girls; the name *house*, to all houses; the name *city*, to all cities. Objects of the same kind form what is called a *class*. The same name can be applied to each object belonging to the same class. The names *boy*, *girl*, *house*, and *city* are called *common nouns*, because they can be applied to any one of a class of objects.

2. A common noun is a name which may be applied to any one of a class of objects; as, *bird*, *door*, *lightning*.

Can the name *John* be applied to all boys? It cannot. Why? Because boys have different names, such as *Charles*, *Frank*, *Samuel*, *Clarence*. Why are boys called by different names? In order to distinguish one from another, or to distinguish a particular boy from the rest of the boys in the school, or in the world.

Can the name *city* be applied to all cities? It can. Is the name *Chicago* applied to all cities? It is not. Why? Because it is the name of a particular city. That is correct; and the names given to particular objects to distinguish them from the rest of their class, are called *proper nouns*.

3. A proper noun is the name of some particular person, place, people, or thing; as, *Susan*, *Rome*, *American*, *Mars*.

What kind of noun is *plow*? It is a common noun. Why? Because it can be applied to all plows.

What kind of noun is *New York*? It is a proper noun. Why? It is the name of a particular city.

Rem. 1—Proper nouns should commence with capital letters. A common noun should commence with a small letter, unless it is the first word of a sentence or is a word of special importance. The words *I* and *O* should always be capital letters.

Write the names of five kinds of fruit; of three kinds of grain; of five articles of clothing; of five games; of five virtues or spiritual fruits; of six farming implements; of four trades; of six towns in your state; of six large cities; of five large rivers; of five mountains; of seven of your schoolmates.

What are the words you have written? Why? Tell which are *common* and which are *proper* nouns.

*Tell which are **common** and which are **proper** nouns in the following list.*

Rain	Organ	Church	Vesuvius
Barn	Boston	Temple	Israel
April	Lesson	Augusta	Black Sea
Hour	College	Volcano	Lake Erie
Snow	Minute	Railroad	Indianapolis
Sarah	Steeple	Thunder	Niagara Falls

Rem. 2—Common nouns, when in a tabulated list of words as above, may begin with capital letters, as if each began a sentence.

*Point out all the nouns in your reading lesson, and tell which are **common** and which are **proper** nouns, using the following model.*

MODEL

"Cicero was an orator."

Cicero is a *noun*; it is a name: *proper*; it is the name of a particular person. **Orator** is a *noun*; (why?): *common*; it may be applied to any one of a class of objects.

Questions—What is a noun? How many classes of nouns are there? What is a common noun? Give examples. What is a proper noun? Give examples. Which class should commence with capital letters? When should common nouns commence with capital letters?

8. NUMBER

Does the word *fan* denote one object, or more than one? It denotes only one object. Does the word *fans* denote one object, or more than one? It denotes more than one object.

That is right. When a noun denotes just one object, it is said to be in the *singular number*.

1. The **singular number** denotes only one object.

When a noun denotes more than one object, it is said to be in the *plural number*.

2. The **plural number** denotes more than one object.

The last sound in the word *fan* readily unites with the sound represented by the letter *s*, and its plural is formed by adding *s* to the singular. The plural of any noun ending with a sound that will readily unite with the sound represented by *s*, is formed by adding *s* to the singular.

The plural of any word ending with a sound that will not readily unite with the sound represented by *s*, is formed by adding *es* to the singular, when the singular does not end with *e*; as, *church*, *church-es*; *cross*, *cross-es*.

These are two ways of forming plurals. There are many other ways. Nouns ending in *f* or *fe* usually change these endings to *ves*; those ending in *y*, with a vowel before it, add *s*; those ending in *y*, with a consonant before it, change *y* to *i* and add *es*; those ending in *o*, with a consonant before it, add *es*. A few nouns are alike in both numbers; as, *sheep*, *deer*, *trout*, *vermin*. Letters, figures, marks, and signs add *'s*; as, *b's*, *6's*, **'s*, *&'s*.

Write the **plurals** *of the following nouns:*

Ox	City	Desk	Alley	Street	School
Girl	Fish	Road	Child	House	Money
Boy	Man	Folly	Wind	Pencil	Wagon
Calf	Rose	Book	Knife	Vessel	Woman
Box	Plow	Chair	Fence	Potato	Monkey

Note—The teacher should assist the pupil in writing the plurals of some of these words. They ought not to be required to remember and apply a large number of rules. The plural forms must be learned by practice in writing them.

Questions—What does the singular number denote? The plural number? Mention some of the ways of forming the plural number.

9. ABBREVIATIONS

I

"Dr. Vinton is a brother of Gen. Vinton, and the father of Mrs. Noble."

In this sentence, the first word is *Doctor*; but in writing it the first and last letters only have been used. This is a short way of writing a word, and it is called an **abbreviation**.

The word *General* is also abbreviated, the first three letters only being used. In abbreviating the word *Mistress*, all the letters are omitted except the first, the fifth, and the last.

A period should be placed after an abbreviation.

Rem.—Abbreviations generally begin with capital letters.

Write the following abbreviations and their equivalents.

Dr.	Doctor	Esq.	Esquire
Mr.	Mister	Gov.	Governor
Cr.	Credit	Rev.	Reverend
St.	Saint *or* Street	Hon.	Honorable
Mt.	Mount	Prof.	Professor
Col.	Colonel	Pres.	President
Gen.	General	Mrs.	Mistress
Maj.	Major	Atty.	Attorney
Lieut.		Capt.	Captain
or Lt.	Lieutenant	Supt.	Superintendent
Co.	Company	Pfc.	Private, first class

Make the proper abbreviations in the following sentences.

1. Major Whipple lives in Saint Louis. 2. Attorney Moses Johnson, Esquire, is an uncle of Professor Collins. 3. Lieutenant Wilson is a guest of Superintendent Furness. 4. Doctor Metz lives on Wood Street, next door to Colonel Clark. 5. Were Mister Bush and President Reagan in the city today?

II

"N.B.—Wm. Smith, Esq., lives in Utica, N.Y."

In this sentence, the first two letters, "N.B.," are the initials, or first letters, of the Latin words, *nota bene*, and are equivalent to *take notice*. "N.Y." is the abbreviation for *New York*, the first letters of each word being used. In addresses followed by a zip code, abbreviations of states are ordinarily written without periods; as, *Utica, NY 13503*.

Write the following abbreviations and their equivalents. Consult the "Abbreviation" section of your dictionary for more information.

a.m.	Forenoon (*ante meridiem*)	m.	Noon
A.M.	Amplitude modulation (a radio frequency)	p.m.	Afternoon (*post meridiem*)
B.C.	Before Christ	A.D.	In the year of our Lord (*anno Domini*)
M.D.	Doctor of medicine	C.O.D.	Collect on delivery
P.O.	Post Office	M	Thousand
P.S.	Postscript	lb.	Pound (libra)
R.R.	Railroad	no.	Number
Bbl.	Barrel	Admr.	Administrator

Write the abbreviations for the days of the week.

Write the abbreviations for the months of the year.

Write the abbreviations for the fifty states.

Note—"A.M.," when placed after the name of a person, is equivalent to *Master of Arts*, also written, M.A. "P.M.," when written or printed in a similar manner, is equivalent to *Postmaster*.

The abbreviations for weights and measures should begin with small letters unless they stand alone or at the beginning of sentences. Many abbreviations are Latin equivalents of English words; as, *ante meridiem* for *forenoon*.

Make the proper abbreviations in the following sentences:

1. Take notice—The train will leave at 3 o'clock in the afternoon. 2. Senator Samuel Fish has moved to Buffalo, New York. 3. Send the books to Joel Elkins, Master of Arts, and collect on delivery. 4. My father left for Europe on the seventh of October. 5. Send me four cases, collect on delivery. 6. I will pay you on the sixth day of November.

Questions—What is an abbreviation? How are periods and capitals used in connection with abbreviations?

10. CONTRACTIONS

"Don't fail to come." In writing or printing *don't*, a mark (') is used between *n* and *t*. It is called an *apostrophe*. In an abbreviation or contraction like this, it shows that one or more letters are omitted.

Tell what letters are omitted in the contracted words in these sentences.

1. We're going home. 2. We'll not go with you. 3. I didn't know the answer. 4. I'll help you as soon as I've learned my lesson. 5. We came from o'er the sea. 6. They're both good students. 7. The corporal said, " 'Bout face."

Note—Many contractions have become regular words through customary usage, and so they are seldom considered to be contractions. They are ordinarily written without apostrophes; as, focsle (forecastle), vest (waistcoat), bald (balled), Boston (St. Batolph's town). Most possessives were once contractions; as, John's coat (John his coat).

11. ELEMENTS OF A SENTENCE

In the sentence, "Chalk is white," *chalk* is called the *subject*, for it is that about which something is *said*, or *affirmed*.

1. The **subject** of a proposition is that of which something is affirmed.

White is called the *predicate*, for it is that which is affirmed of the subject *chalk*.

2. The **predicate** of a proposition is that which is affirmed of the subject.

Is is called the *copula*, for it is used to join the predicate to the subject, and the word *copula* means a *link*. The copula also affirms that the predicate belongs to the subject. It is sometimes a group of words; as, *will be*, *shall have been*, etc. A copula may also be called a *linking verb*. Some grammarians consider the copula/linking verb to be a part of the predicate.

3. The **copula** is a word, or group of words, used to join a predicate to a subject and to make an assertion.

In the sentence, "Ice is cold," what is the subject? "**Ice**." Why? Because it is that of which something is affirmed. What is the predicate? "**Cold**." Why? Because it is that which is affirmed of the subject. What is the copula? "**Is**." Why? Because it is the word used to assert the predicate *cold* of the subject *ice*. Why is it called the copula? Because it links or joins the predicate to the subject.

Point out the **subject**, **predicate**, *and* **copula** *in each of the following sentences.*

1. Air is transparent. 2. Iron is heavy. 3. Nero was cruel. 4. Jane has been studious. 5. Walter will be prompt. 6. Mary should be kind. 7. Ellen is unhappy. 8. Martha was cheerful. 9. George should have been industrious.

Point out the nouns in these sentences, and tell which are **common** *and which are* **proper** *nouns.*

Questions—What is the subject of a proposition? The predicate? The copula? What does the word *copula* mean?

12. THE PREDICATE

In the sentence, "Man is mortal," the predicate *mortal* denotes a quality belonging to the subject *man*. Words which express qualities may be called **quality words**.

Nouns may be used as predicates. When they are thus used, they denote *kind* or *class*.

In the sentence, "Horses are animals," what is the subject? "**Horses**." Why? What is the predicate? "**Animals**." Why? What does the word *animals* denote? It denotes the kind or class of beings to which horses belong. What part of speech is it? It is a noun. Why? What is the copula? "**Are**."

Affirm **qualities** *of the following subjects.*

Iron	_____	Trees	_____	Fishes	_____	Oranges	_____
Play	_____	Books	_____	Apples	_____	Marbles	_____
Lead	_____	School	_____	Flowers	_____	Swimming	_____

Model—Oranges are *yellow*.

*Affirm the following qualities of appropriate **subjects**.*

_____	soft	_____	hard	_____	young	_____	opaque
_____	wise	_____	sweet	_____	happy	_____	mellow
_____	blue	_____	round	_____	square	_____	transparent

Model—*Sugar* is *sweet*.

*Affirm **kind** or **class** of the following subjects.*

Gold	_____	Oxen	_____	Sheep	_____	Wheat	_____
Corn	_____	River	_____	Eagles	_____	Houses	_____
Coats	_____	Silver	_____	Tables	_____	Wagons	_____

Model—*Eagles* are *birds*.

Questions—What are quality words? Can they be used as predicates? Give examples. Give an example of a noun used as a predicate.

13. ELEMENTS

We have seen that a sentence is composed of parts. These parts are called *elements*.

1. An **element** is one of the distinct parts of a sentence.

2. The *subject* and the *predicate* are called **principal elements** because no sentence can be formed without them. All other distinct parts of a sentence are called **subordinate elements**. The *copula* is not called an element.

3. **Analysis** is the separation of a sentence into its elements. Any sentence can be so separated.

Analyze the following sentences, using this model.

MODEL

"Iron is heavy."

This is a *sentence*; it is a group of words making complete sense: *declarative*; it states a fact.

Iron is the *subject*; it is that of which something is affirmed: **heavy** is the *predicate*; it is that which is affirmed of the subject: **is** is the *copula*; it joins the predicate to the subject.

Iron | is : heavy

1. Indigo is blue. 2. Flies are insects. 3. Mary was prompt. 4. Boys will be playful. 5. Children should be careful. 6. Men should be prudent. 7. John can be studious. 8. Roses are fragrant. 9. Julius is diligent.

*Point out the **common** and **proper** nouns in the above sentences.*

Questions—What is an element? What are the principal elements? Subordinate elements? What is analysis?

14. COMPOSITION

I

Note—The answers to the questions in this and similar exercises should first be given orally and then written on paper. The first answer should begin with the words, "I see."

Look at the picture, and answer the following questions.

1. What do you see in this picture?
2. What are the boy and the girl doing?
3. Where is the bird's nest?
4. Where is the bird?
5. Why should the children be careful not to touch the eggs?

Read what has been written.

II

1. What do you see in this picture?
2. What is the dog doing?
3. How many rats has he killed already?
4. What are the rats trying to do?
5. Will the dog catch the one that is trying to climb the broom? Why?
6. Where do rats live?
7. What harm do they do?

Read what has been written.

THE VERB

15. ORAL LESSON

In the sentence, "Fish swim," what is the subject? "**Fish**." Why? What is the predicate? "**Swim**." Why? Is there any copula expressed? There is not.

The predicate, then, can be affirmed of the subject *directly*. One word expresses both the copula and the predicate.

A word which can be used to affirm something of a subject is called a *verb*. It usually expresses *action*, *being*, or *state*; as, I *run* denotes action; I *am* denotes being; I *sleep* denotes state.

A **verb** is a word which expresses action, being, or state; as, George *writes*, I *am*, he *dreams*.

What is the word "trot" in the sentence, "Horses trot?" It is a verb. Why? Because it affirms *action* of the subject "horses."

What is the word "stand" in the sentence "Houses stand?" It is a verb. Why? Because it affirms *state* of the subject "houses."

*Write sentences, using the following verbs as **predicates**.*

_____	sail	_____	look	_____	loiter	_____	whine
_____	purr	_____	limp	_____	listen	_____	cackle
_____	run	_____	mow	_____	study	_____	gobble
_____	sing	_____	howl	_____	neigh	_____	trust
_____	play	_____	walk	_____	stand	_____	scream
_____	reap	_____	work	_____	recite	_____	whistle

Model—Birds *sing*.

*Point out all the **verbs** in your reading lesson.*

Questions—What is a verb? What does it usually express? Give the directions for writing sentences. (See Section 3.)

16. CLASSES OF VERBS

In the sentence, "Boys study grammar," the word "grammar" is required to complete the meaning of the predicate "study." That which tells *what* the boys study, completes its meaning, and is called an *objective element*, or *object*.

1. An **objective element** is a word or a group of words which completes the meaning of a verb.

Those verbs which require the addition of an object to complete their meaning, are called *transitive verbs*.

2. A **transitive verb** requires the addition of an object to complete its meaning.

Ex.—"Columbus *discovered* America." The verb "discovered" requires the addition of some word, as "America," to complete its meaning, and is, therefore, *transitive*.

Rem.—The object of a transitive verb is not always expressed; but some word different from the subject can always be made its object.

In the sentence, "Clarence walks," no word is required to complete the meaning of the verb "walks." Those verbs which do not require the addition of an object to complete their meaning are called *intransitive verbs*.

3. An **intransitive verb** does not require the addition of an object to complete its meaning.

Ex.—"Horses *run*." The verb "run" does not require the addition of an object to complete its meaning. It is, therefore, *intransitive*.

Rem.—Some verbs are transitive in one sense and intransitive in another sense. To determine whether a verb can be used both transitively and intransitively consult a dictionary.

The copula is always a verb.

4. A **copulative verb** is used to join or link a predicate to a subject and to make an assertion.

Ex.—"Lambs *are* playful." The verb "are" is used to join the predicate "playful" to the subject "lambs." It is, therefore, a *copulative* or *linking* verb.

*Write seven sentences containing **transitive** verbs.*

Model—John ate pie.

*Write seven sentences containing **intransitive** verbs.*

Models—Houses *stand*. Boys *swim*.

*Write seven sentences containing **copulative** verbs.*

Model—The weather *was* warm.

*Write sentences, using the following nouns as **objective elements**.*

_____ cars	_____ grass	_____ books	_____ churches
_____ laws	_____ wood	_____ wheat	_____ elephants
_____ lions	_____ boats	_____ letters	_____ geography
_____ trees	_____ debts	_____ pictures	_____ mountains

Model—Fire burns *wood*.

Analyze the following sentences, using this model.

MODEL

"Scholars learn lessons."

This is a *sentence*; (why?): *declarative*: (why?).

Scholars is the *subject*; (why?): **learn** is the *predicate*; (why?). "Learn" is modified by **lessons**, an *objective element*.

Scholars | learn | lessons

1. Dogs hunt rabbits. 2. Jane studies botany. 3. Eli drives horses. 4. Horses draw wagons. 5. Men build houses. 6. Farmers sow grain. 7. Merchants sell goods. 8. Haste makes waste. 9. Soldiers fight battles. 10. Cats catch mice.

Point out the verbs in the following sentences, using the models.

MODELS

I. "The nights are chilly."

Are is a *verb*; it denotes being: *copulative*; it joins the predicate to the subject.

II. "Corn grows."

Grows is a *verb*; (why?): *intransitive*; it does not require an object to complete its meaning.

III. "Horses draw wagons."

Draw is a *verb*; (why?): *transitive*; it requires an object to complete its meaning.

1. Viola blushed. 2. Stephen was a martyr. 3. Tools may be useful. 4. Merchants sell goods. 5. Carpenters build houses. 6. Fish swim. 7. James is sick. 8. John should be careful. 9. Dogs kill sheep. 10. Henry struck William.

*Point out the nouns in these sentences and tell which are **common** and which are **proper** nouns.*

Questions—What is an objective element? A transitive verb? An intransitive verb? A copulative verb? Is the object of a transitive verb always expressed? Give a sentence in which it is not expressed.

17. INCORRECT LANGUAGE

Caution I—Do not use **saw** for **seen** or **went** for **gone** after *has, have, has been*, or *have been*.

Ex.—1. I have saw a fine horse today. 2. The little boy has went into the woods. 3. George has went there several times. 4. Have you saw Mr. Olds today?

Caution II—Do not use **see** or **seen** for **saw** in expressing past time.

Ex.—1. Hiram see a flock of wild turkeys yesterday. 2. I seen a dog running after a fox. 3. I know John was whispering; I seen him. 4. It is the largest peach I ever see.

Caution III—Do not use **done** for **did** or **come** for **came** in expressing past time.

Ex.—1. He done his work well yesterday. 2. My father come home last week. 3. I done my task before Eli come.

Caution IV—Do not use **is, was,** or **has been** as the copula or predicate of a sentence whose subject denotes more than one object.

Ex.—1. The horse and the cow is in the stable. 2. Weasels was plenty around there. 3. Debbie and Sandy has been here. 4. We was very much surprised. 5. Are you sure that they was here?

Caution V—Do not use **was** for **were** as the copula or predicate of a sentence whose subject is *you.*

Ex.—1. You was there, we know. 2. Perhaps you was trying to hide somewhere.

18. SENTENCE MAKING

In the sentence, "John and Brad went to town," two words are used as the subject—what are they? *John* and *Brad*. In the sentence, "John, Brad, and Eddie went to town," how many nouns are used as the subject? Three— *John*, *Brad*, and *Eddie*.

Observe that in the first sentence the two nouns used as the subject are joined by the word *and*. There is no comma (,) after the first word. Observe, also, that in the second sentence, there is a comma after the first two nouns— *John* and *Brad*.

When several words are used in the same way, they are said to be *of the same kind*, or *rank*, and they form what is called a *series*. When more than two words are thus used to form a series, they should be separated by commas. Write the following rules for punctuation on your papers and commit them to memory.

Rule I—Three or more words of the same kind or rank, used together, should be separated by commas.

Rule II—Two words of the same kind or rank, used together, are not usually separated by commas but are connected by *and*, *or*, or some similar word.

Rem.—When two words of the same rank, used together, are not connected by *and*, *or*, or some similar word, they are usually separated by commas.

Arrange the following words into sentences.

1. Houses, barns, build, and, garages, carpenters. 2. Raise, wheat, corn, farmers, barley, and. 3. In, oranges, Hawaii, lemons, grow, and, pineapples. 4. Metals, gold, are, silver, precious, and. 5. Mary, Susan, cousins, are, Ada, and. 6. New York, cities, and, large, Philadelphia, are, San Francisco.

Note—In writing these sentences, observe carefully the directions given in the two rules for the use of the comma.

Fill the blanks in the following exercises.

1. I have _____ _____ _____ in my desk.

2. _____ _____ _____ _____ are wild animals.

3. A merchant sells _____ _____ _____ _____.

4. I can buy _____ _____ _____ _____ from a grocer.

5. Have you seen ___ ___ ___ ___?

6. ___ ___ ___ are ___ in Colorado.

7. I can see ___ ___ ___ from my window.

8. Violets _____ _____ _____ are _____ flowers.

9. _____ and four and _____ and six equal _____.

19. COMPOSITION

Tell what these children are doing. Give them names. Tell whether the two standing together are at home or at the home of the little girl holding the doll.

Tell how old you think the little girl is that has a basket on her arm. How much older is the little boy?

Write a story about three children that played Store one afternoon.

Write a story about a brother and a sister that spent a day with their cousin who lived in the country. Tell what games they played.

Write a story about three girls at home one afternoon. Tell how they spent the afternoon, what books they read, what games they played, etc.

Write a description of a tree house you would like to build. Tell whether you would have a club who could use it, or if it would be open to all children.

THE ADJECTIVE

20. ORAL LESSON

When quality words are joined to nouns by copulas, they are said to be *predicated* of those nouns.

They may be written or printed in connection with nouns, without being joined to them by copulas; thus: *white* chalk, *sour* apples, a *square* table, *good* boys.

When thus used, they describe or restrict the meaning of nouns, but are not *predicated* of them.

Words that do not express quality may be used as modifiers of nouns. In the sentences, "*This* book is heavy," "*That* book is light," "*Two* boys were sick," "*Three* boys were busy," the words, *this*, *that*, *two*, and *three*, are modifiers of the nouns that follow them, but they do not express any quality. *This* and *that* point out the nouns to which they belong; *two* and *three* denote number.

Those words which modify nouns by expressing quality, pointing them out, or denoting number, are called *adjectives*.

1. An **adjective** is a word used to describe or define a noun.

2. There are two classes of adjectives: *descriptive* and *definitive*.

All quality words are *descriptive adjectives*.

3. A **descriptive adjective** describes a noun by expressing some quality belonging to it; as, *good*, *white*.

Pointing-out words and number words are *definitive adjectives*.

4. A **definitive adjective** limits or defines a noun without expressing any of its qualities; as *this*, *few*.

Rem.—Most adjectives derived from proper nouns, should commence with capitals; as, *American* cotton, *French* customs. As time passes, proper nouns may become common nouns, however. For example, *chinaware*, meaning "porcelain dishes," is no longer capitalized, since most china no longer comes from China.

Place a noun after each of the following adjectives.

dry	_____	dirty	_____	rough	_____	Spanish	_____
bad	_____	light	_____	round	_____	healthy	_____
soft	_____	moist	_____	square	_____	pleasant	_____
good	_____	warm	_____	smooth	_____	Australian	_____

Models—*Smooth* ice. *Clean* hands.

What kind of adjectives are these? Why?

Place a noun after each of the following adjectives.

that	_____	some	_____	latter	_____	yonder	_____
four	_____	many	_____	either	_____	neither	_____
such	_____	these	_____	certain	_____	another	_____
each	_____	those	_____	various	_____	fourfold	_____

Models—*Much* money. *Several* books.

What kind of adjectives are these? Why?

*Point out the **adjectives** in the following sentences, using this model.*

MODEL

"Fearful storms sweep over these islands."

Fearful is an *adjective*; it is a word which modifies the meaning of a noun: *descriptive*; it denotes a quality. **These** is an *adjective*; *definitive*; it defines without denoting any quality.

1. Both horses are lame. 2. Ripe peaches are plentiful. 3. Large houses are expensive. 4. You may take either road. 5. That boy has a kind father. 6. Every man carried a square box. 7. This lesson is hard. 8. The brave soldier received a severe wound. 9. That large cat caught this brown mouse.

*Point out the **nouns** and **verbs** in the above sentences.*

*Point out the **adjectives** in your reading lesson.*

Questions—What is an adjective? A descriptive adjective? A definitive adjective? What adjectives should commence with capitals?

THE ARTICLE

21. ORAL LESSON

When we say, "*A* horse was stolen," *a* denotes that *one* horse is meant, but it does not point out any particular horse.

When we say "*The* horse was stolen," *the* denotes that a particular horse is meant.

The words "*A*" and "*The*" in these sentences are definitive adjectives, because they limit nouns without denoting any of their qualities. They are also called **articles**.

A and *an* are different forms of the same word. *A* is used when the following word begins with a subvocal or aspirate; *an*, when the following word begins with a vocal, also known as a vowel sound.

1. **The** is called the **definite article**, because it points out definitely the object which it restricts.

2. **A** or **an** is called the **indefinite article**, because it restricts in an indefinite or general manner.

Place a or an before the following words, and tell why it should be used.

_____ egg	_____ hour	_____ hearth	_____ memory
_____ ode	_____ eagle	_____ humor	_____ measure
_____ cart	_____ stand	_____ orange	_____ opossum
_____ goat	_____ house	_____ turkey	_____ elephant
_____ oven	_____ honor	_____ vulture	_____ advantage

Use a or an instead of the dashes in the following sentences, and tell why it should be used.

1. Self control is _____ virtue. 2. The house stands on _____ hill. 3._____ loud report was heard. 4. Life is but _____ vapor. 5. He is _____ honest man. 6. He has _____ ax to grind. 7. Father has bought _____ horse. 8. My being _____ child, was _____ plea for my admission.

Use the proper articles instead of the dashes in the following sentences.

1. Such _____ law is _____ disgrace to any state. 2. Repeat _____ first four lines in concert. 3. Love took up _____ harp of life and smote on all _____ chords with might. 4. _____ fox is cunning. 5. _____ days are calm. 6. _____ wise son maketh _____ glad father.

*Point out the **articles** in your reading lesson, using this model.*

MODEL

"The man was riding in a convertible."

The is a *definite article*; it points out definitely the object which it restricts. **A** is an *indefinite article*; it restricts in an indefinite or general manner.

Questions—What words are called articles? Which is the definite article? The indefinite article? When is *a* used? When is *an* used?

22. SENTENCE MAKING

I

Write sentences containing the following words, supplying words, where necessary, to make complete sense.

1. Flowers, the, garden. 2. Fish, sea. 3. Nests, birds. 4. Winter, go, robins, where. 5. Quarts, how, gallon. 6. Five, thirty. 7. Columbus, Ohio. 8. Lion, man, the. 9. Let, book, me. 10. Dog, that, cross, is, ugly, and. 11. I, in, large, live, a, roomy, house, brick. 12. Col. Smith, prudent, man, brave, and, honorable, a, is. 13. Sugar, grocer, soap, coffee, a, sells.

Fill the blanks in these exercises, carefully choosing words.

1. ____ ____ America.

2. San Francisco ____ ____ California.

3. ____ ____ in the winter.

4. I have ____ ____ lesson.

5. ____ ____ when the ice is smooth.

6. Where do the birds ____ ?

II

In the sentence, "I saw a little old man," *little* and *old* are adjectives, but they are not separated by commas. The expression *old man* is modified by *little*, and not just the noun *man* alone. When an adjective and a noun form a single expression in this way, the adjective is not separated by a comma from another adjective placed before it.

Punctuate the following sentences properly.

1. The kind old man took the poor child in his arms. 2. Plain honest truth needs no artificial covering. 3. Mary is a gentle sensible and well-behaved girl. 4. The good man was loved esteemed and respected. 5. His large old-fashioned spectacles frightened the child. 6. That little mischievous boy is my nephew.

23. INCORRECT LANGUAGE

Caution I—Do not use **a** before vowel sounds, or **an** before sub-vocals and aspirates.

Ex.—1. An hundred cents make one dollar. 2. There should be an universal rejoicing. 3. This is a open country. 4. Henry is a honest lad.

Caution II—Do not use **these** or **those** before a noun in the singular number.

Ex.—1. I don't like these kind of apples. 2. These sort of people are good neighbors. 3. Those yoke of oxen belong to me.

Note—In each of these samples the nouns (kind, sort, yoke) are singular because they speak of a single class (one kind, though many apples; one sort, though many people; only one yoke, though two oxen).

Caution III—Do not use **them** for **those**; **this here** for **this**; or **that there** for **that**.

Ex—1. Look at them tramps. 2. Do you live in this here house? 3. That there girl is wearing a blue dress.

24. COMPOSITION

What do you see in this picture? What can be seen through the window? Is the storm approaching the house where the girl is, or has it passed it? Why do you think so? Does the picture represent a morning or an evening scene?

Write a description of the prominent objects to be seen from the door of the schoolhouse—also, a description of anything that may occur while you are looking at these objects.

Describe what may be seen through a window or door of your home.

Describe what may be seen from various places near your home—also, what may have occurred during your visits to those places.

THE PARTICIPLE

25. ORAL LESSON

"James saw the man plowing."

What is the subject of this sentence? Why? What is the predicate? Why? What is the objective element? Why? What words limit or restrict "man"? The words "the" and "plowing." What does the word "plowing" denote? It tells what the man was doing. Does it *affirm* anything of man? It does not: it modifies it like an adjective.

The word "plowing," then, partakes of the properties of both a verb and an adjective. Like a verb, it expresses *action*: like an adjective, it *modifies* a *noun*. Because it partakes of the properties of two parts of speech, it is called a *participle*, which means *partaking of*.

1. A **participle** is a word derived from a verb, partaking of the properties of a verb and of an adjective or a noun.

When we say, "The boy is *writing*," the participle "writing" denotes a *continuance* of the act: the boy is *continuing to write*.

When we say, "The letter is *written*," the participle "written" denotes a *completion* of the act: the writing of the letter is *finished*.

When we say, "*Having written* the letter, he mailed it," the words "having written" denote that the writing of the letter was *completed before the time represented by the verb* "mailed."

2. There are three participles: the *present*, the *perfect*, and the *compound*.

3. The **present participle** denotes the continuance of action, being, or state; as, *loving, being loved*.

The *present participle* always ends in *ing*. This participle may be used as an adjective. It is then placed before the noun it modifies, as in the sentence, "Look at the *twinkling* stars," and is called a *participial adjective*. It may also be used as a noun, as in the sentence, "I am fond of *reading*."

4. The **perfect participle** denotes the completion of action, being, or state; as, *loved, been, lived*.

The *perfect participle* usually ends in *d* or *ed*, but frequently in *n*, *en*, or *t*. This participle is frequently used as an adjective but never as a noun.

5. The **compound participle** denotes the completion of action, being, or state at or before the time represented by the principal verb; as, "*Having learned* the lesson, he recited it."

Rem.—The "principal verb" is the verb used as copula or predicate of the sentence in which the compound participle is found.

The compound participle is formed by placing *having* or *having been* before a perfect participle, or *having been* before a present participle; as, *having learned, having been learned, having been learning.*

Give the present, perfect, and compound participles of the following verbs.

go	spell	take	suffer	answer
sit	hope	make	enjoy	demand
see	grow	learn	recite	enchant
help	come	write	arrive	resemble
find	paint	study	inquire	reconcile

Point out all the participles in the following exercises, using these models.

MODELS

I. "The boy, laughing, ran away."

Laughing is a *participle*; it is a word derived from the verb *laugh*, and partakes of the properties of a verb and of an adjective: *present*; it denotes the *continuance* of an act.

II. "The lesson, studied carefully, was recited."

Studied is a *participle*; (why?): *perfect*; it denotes *completion*.

III. "Having recited, we were dismissed."

Having recited is a *participle*; (why?): *compound*; it denotes the *completion of an act before the time represented by the principal verb.*

1. Look at Dash playing with Rose. 2. I send you this note, written in haste, hoping it will reach you before you leave town. 3. Here it comes sparkling, and there it lies darkling. 4. Having finished the task assigned me, I will rest awhile. 5. The boy passed on, whistling as before. 6. The fort, situated on a high hill, was captured at daybreak. 7. I see men as trees, walking.

Questions—What is a participle? The present participle? How does it end? The perfect participle? How does it usually end? The compound participle? How is it formed?

26. THE PARTICIPIAL NOUN

In the sentence, "I like skating," what part of speech is *skating*? It is a noun. Why? It is a *name*, the name of an action.

That is correct. It is a noun; but, as it expresses action, and is derived from the verb "skate," it is called a **participial noun**. A participial noun is also a common noun; but it need not be called such in parsing. A participial noun ending in *ing* is also known as a **gerund**.

*Point out the **participial nouns** in the following exercises, using this model.*

MODEL

"Miss Gray teaches writing."

This is a *sentence, declarative.*

Writing is a noun; (why?): participial; it is derived from the verb "write," and partakes of the properties of a verb and a noun.

1. He was in danger of losing his life. 2. Let there be no more running and jumping in the house. 3. These strawberries are of my own raising. 4. They could not avoid being discovered.

*Point out the **participles** and **participial nouns** in the following exercises.*

1. John would have avoided meeting him if he could have done so without being called a coward. 2. Looking over the wall, we saw a fox caught in a trap. 3. Seeing is believing. 4. The poor woman, wringing her hands, stood at the door. 5. Who told you of my being here? 6. Do you see the teacher pointing his finger at us?

Read the following three times, then reproduce it from memory.

THE DOG AND THE PARTRIDGE

As I was hunting with a young pointer, the dog ran on a brood of very small partridges. The old bird cried, fluttered, and ran tumbling along just before the spaniel's nose till she had drawn him to a considerable distance. Then she took wing and flew still farther off, but not out of the field. Seeing this, the dog returned to me near the place where the young birds lay concealed in the grass. The old bird no sooner perceived this, than she flew back to us, settled just before the dog's nose, and by rolling and tumbling about, drew off his attention from her young, and thus preserved her brood a second time.

27. COMPOSITION

Where do you think these boys have been? What are the man and the little boy talking about? Tell what time of day you think it is. Are the children going to a picnic or coming home from one? Write a description of what you think they have been doing.

Write a story about a drive to a park, a lake, or the seashore.

Write a composition about the last picnic that you attended.

Write a story about a foolhardy boy that was hurt at a picnic by falling from a tree which he was told not to climb.

Describe a fishing trip. Describe a walk along the bank of a river. Tell what you saw.

THE PRONOUN

28. ORAL LESSON

"John put John's hat on John's head."

Is this a correct sentence? It is not. What word is unnecessarily repeated? "John's." How should the sentence be written? It should be written, "John put *his* hat on *his* head." What word is here used instead of John's? "His." This word is called a *pronoun*, which means *instead of a noun*.

1. A **pronoun** is a word used instead of a noun; as, *he* runs, *she* sings, *they* listen.

Point out the pronouns in these sentences.

1. He is your uncle. 2. His dog worried our cat. 3. She lost the book which he gave her. 4. Did you tell me who they are? 5. It cannot find its way out. 6. Were you with them? 7. Yes, I was with them and can tell you what they said. 8. It was the dog that died. 9. Sarah cannot find her book. 10. Who will find it for her?

29. THE ADJECTIVE ELEMENT

I

In the sentence, "Small lakes are abundant," what word modifies "lakes"? The adjective "small."

In the sentence, "John's hat is torn," what word modifies "hat"? The noun "John's." In what manner does it modify "hat"? It denotes that it is the hat which John owns.

In the sentence, "Mr. Jones, the mason, builds chimneys," what word modifies "Mr. Jones"? The noun "mason." In what manner does it modify "Mr. Jones"? It tells his trade, or business.

These modifying words are called *adjective elements*, because they modify nouns.

1. An **adjective element** or **adjective** is a word, or group of words, which modifies a noun.

In the sentence, "Ripe peaches are plentiful," what element is "ripe"? It is an adjective. Why? Because it modifies the noun "peaches."

In the sentence, "This boy has six peaches," what elements are "this" and "six"? They are adjectives. Why?

Write five sentences, modifying their subjects by **descriptive** *adjectives.*

Model—*Cold* weather is unpleasant.

*Write five sentences, modifying their subjects by **definitive** adjectives.*

Model—*Both* horses are lame.

II

In the sentence, "John's hat is torn," the noun "John's" is called a *possessive*, because it denotes *ownership*. A possessive always modifies a noun denoting a different object from itself and sometimes denotes *kind* or *authorship* instead of *ownership*; as, *Ray's Arithmetic*.

1. **A possessive** is a noun or pronoun used to modify a noun *different in meaning* from itself. When a noun or pronoun is used as a possessive, it is said to be in the *possessive case*.

Rem. 1—A possessive may be modified by another possessive and by an adjective. In the sentence, "John's brother's bike is broken," the possessive "brother's" is modified by "John's."

Rem. 2—The apostrophe (') is used to show that a noun is a possessive.

Rem. 3—When a noun denotes but one object, the letter *s* follows the apostrophe; as in *John's, Moses's*. The apostrophe only is used after a few words; as in *conscience' sake, goodness' sake, Jesus' sake*, etc.

Rem. 4—When the noun denotes more than one object or person, and ends with *s*, the apostrophe alone is used, as in the *ladies'* room.

Rem. 5—When the noun denotes more than one object and does not end with *s*, the apostrophe is usually followed by *s*, as in *men's*.

Note—Illustrate these rules by writing on the blackboard appropriate examples of plural nouns in the possessive case. The examples should always be used in sentences. Show, also, that the apostrophe is never used in writing the possessive case of a pronoun or to form a plural. For example, do not write, "Banana's are 49¢ a pound."

Model—*Eli's* uncle is rich. *His* head is bald.

*Write five sentences, modifying their subjects by **possessives**.*

*Point out the **possessives** in the following sentences.*

1. Your father's brother is my uncle. 2. Mr. Eddy sells children's shoes. 3. Our farm once belonged to your grandfather. 4. Her doll's dress was soiled. 5. We met on the boys' playground. 6. Did you ride in the ladies' car? 7. The horse's foot is lame. 8. Have you read Andrews's *Geology*?

*Correct the **errors** in the following sentences.*

1. The flag was fastened to the ox' horn. 2. The canary is not in it's cage. 3. The vessels sail's are spread. 4. Alice' lesson is learned. 5. The hook caught in the boys' coat. 6. We then went into the ladie's parlor.

III

In the sentence, "The nest of the bird is very small," what word may be used instead of the group "of the bird"? The word "bird's." What is that word? It is a *possessive*.

That is correct. A group of words beginning with "of" may frequently be used instead of a possessive.

*Substitute **groups** for the possessives in the following sentences.*

1. I grasped the boy's hand. 2. Daniel was in the lion's den. 3. The vessel's owner was drowned. 4. Have you found the fox's den? 5. We were startled by the lightning's flash. 6. Were you at home when the barn's roof was blown off? 7. An owl's hoot was heard.

*Substitute **possessives** for the groups beginning with "of" in the following sentences.*

1. The head of the horse was hurt. 2. We rested by the bank of the river. 3. The house of the squirrel was a hollow tree. 4. The hunters came to the den of a tiger. 5. The owner of the dog was much surprised.

IV

In the sentence, "Mr. Jones the mason builds chimneys," the noun "mason" is called an *appositive*. An appositive always denotes the same object as that denoted by the noun it modifies, and usually expresses *rank*, *office*, or *business*.

1. An **appositive** is a word, or group of words, used to modify a noun or pronoun by denoting the same object.

An appositive is usually placed after the noun or pronoun with which it is in apposition. Thus, in the sentence, "The emperor Nero was a cruel tyrant," "Nero" is in apposition with "emperor."

Rule—An appositive is usually set off by a comma unless it is unmodified or modified by *the* only.

*Write five sentences, modifying their subjects or objects by **appositives**.*

Models—Mr. Tod the *mason* died yesterday. I have seen Mr. Smith the *engineer*.

*Point out the **appositives** in the following sentences.*

1. Mr. Whitcomb the lawyer is out of town. 2. Milton the poet was blind. 3. Stephenson, the famous engineer, lived in England. 4. Have you seen Mr. Hicks, the man who sells strawberries? 5. I am reading the speeches of the statesman Daniel Webster. 6. Washington, the capital of the United States, is situated on the Potomac.

Analyze the following sentences, using these models.

MODELS

I. "Sweet sounds soothe the ear."

This is a *sentence, declarative*.
Sounds is the subject; **soothe**, the predicate. "Sounds" is modified by **sweet**, an adjective; "soothe," by **ear**, an object; "ear," by **the**, an adjective.

```
sounds | soothe | ear
  | Sweet        | the
```

II. "Frank's father is a merchant."

This is a *sentence, declarative*.
Father is the subject; **merchant**, the predicate. "Father" is modified by **Frank's**, an adjective element; "merchant," by **a**, an adjective.

III. "Milton the poet was blind."

This is a *sentence, declarative*.
Milton is the subject; **blind**, the predicate; **was** is the copula. "Milton" is modified by **poet**, an adjective element; "poet," by **the**, an adjective element.

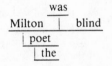

```
          was
Milton  |  blind
  | poet
     | the
```

Note—An alternative, simplified diagramming method is illustrated below.

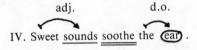

IV. Sweet sounds soothe the ear .

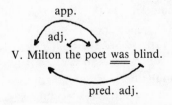

V. Milton the poet was blind.

An entire sentence can thus be written on one line on the board without disjointing it. Underline verbs twice and simple subjects once. Circle all objects and put brackets around prepositional phrases and modifying clauses. Show relationships with arrows and labels.

1. Clarence is a good scholar. 2. Charles found an old knife. 3. Helen's mother is sick. 4. Miss Young the milliner is dead. 5. Mary studied her spelling lesson.

6. The thief stole father's horse. 7. The sheriff caught Hobbs the burglar. 8. Five boys earned three dollars each. 9. Both vessels have sailed. 10. Each boy earned a dollar.

11. Several scholars were tardy. 12. Few men escaped. 13. Many men died. 14. Mr. Snooks the grocer boards Mr. Sears the tailor. 15. John's bat is broken.

Point out the verbs, participles, and adjectives in these exercises.

Questions—What is a pronoun? What is an adjective element? Can nouns be used as adjective elements?

What is a possessive? Give the directions for writing possessives. What is an appositive? Give the rule for writing appositives.

30. PERSONAL PRONOUNS

In the sentences, "*I* write," "*You* read," "*They* study," what are the words "*I*," "*you*,"' and "*they*"? They are pronouns. Why? Because they are used instead of nouns—"I," instead of the name of the person speaking; "you," instead of the name of the person spoken to; "they," instead of the names of the persons spoken of.

The name of a person speaking, or a pronoun used instead of that name, is said to be of the *first person*.

1. The **first person** denotes the speaker.

The name of a person spoken to, or a pronoun used instead of that name, is said to be of the *second person*.

2. The **second person** denotes the person spoken to.

The name of a person or object spoken of, or a pronoun used instead of that name, is said to be of the *third person*.

3. The **third person** denotes the person or object spoken of.

Those pronouns which show by their form whether the nouns which they represent are of the first, second, or third person are called *personal pronouns*.

4. **Personal pronouns** both represent nouns and show by their form whether they are of the first, second, or third person.

Rem. 1—The personal pronouns are *I, you, he, she, it, we, our, us, my, mine, your, his, him, her, its, they, their, them, myself, himself*, etc.

Rem. 2—*Thou, thee, ye, thy*, and *thine* are old pronoun forms found in the Bible and Shakespeare. Students should *recognize* these, since they appear frequently in literature, but need not learn to *use* them.

*Point out all the **personal pronouns** in the following sentences.*

1. Thou callest. 2. I come. 3. She studies. 4. I like her. 5. They are honest. 6. Her lesson was learned. 7. I borrowed his books. 8. They have sold their farms. 9. You should study your lesson. 10. Ye are the people. 11. It cannot find its master. 12. Thy fame hath preceded thee.

*Analyze the foregoing sentences, and point out the **nouns** and **verbs**, using these models.*

MODELS

I. "It is he."

This is a *sentence, declarative*.
It is the subject; **he** is the predicate; **is** is the copula.

II. "He has lost his book."

This is a *sentence, declarative*.
He is the subject; **has lost**, the predicate. "Has lost," is modified by **book**, an object; and "book" by **his**, an adjective.

III. "Their horses exhausted themselves."

This is a *sentence, declarative*.
Horses is the subject; **exhausted**, the predicate. "Horses" is modified by **their**, an adjective element, and "exhausted" by **themselves**, an object.

*Substitute appropriate **pronouns** for the blanks in the following sentences.*

1. Steven died a martyr to ____ faith. 2. ____ house to ____ was a strange land. 3. ____ said of ____ son, " ____ is ____ brother." 4. Let there be no strife betwixt ____ and ____. 5. Lend ____ ____ pen till ____ write ____ exercises. 6. How much ____ missed ____ brother and _____ sister. 7. _____ say _____ are _____ friends. 8. ____ asked ____ to visit ____. 9. Would ____ think ____ right for _____ to neglect _____ garden?

*Write five sentences using personal pronouns as **subjects**.*

Model—*We* are students.

*Write five sentences using personal pronouns as **subjects** and **predicates**.*

Model—*It* was *she*.

Write five sentences using personal pronouns as **objects**.

Model—Henry admires *them*.

Write five sentences using personal pronouns as **adjective elements**.

Model—*His* book is in *his* hand.

Point out the **personal pronouns** *in your reading lesson, using this model.*

MODEL

"His book is on my desk."

His is a *pronoun*; it is a word used instead of a noun: *personal*; it represents a noun, and shows that it is of the *third person*.

My is a *pronoun*, *personal*; it represents a noun, and shows that it is of the *first person*.

Questions—What is a pronoun? A personal pronoun? Name some of the personal pronouns. What is the first person? The second person? The third person?

31. POSSESSIVE PRONOUNS

In the sentence, "This house is ours," what is the subject? "House." Why? What is the predicate? "Ours." Why? It is that which is affirmed of the subject. What is the copula? "Is."

What modifies "house"? "This," an adjective element. What words can be used instead of "ours"? *Our house.* What does the pronoun "our" denote? It denotes that we *own* the house.

"Ours," then, is used to denote both the possessor and the thing possessed. In this sentence, it represents both "our" and "house." Because it does this, it is called a *possessive pronoun*.

Possessive pronouns are words used to represent both the possessor and the thing possessed. The possessive pronouns are *mine*, *his*, *hers*, *ours*, *yours*, *theirs*, *our own*, etc.

In the sentence, "That book is his," what is the predicate? "His." Why? What does it represent? It represents the words *his book*. What is it? It is a possessive pronoun. Why? Because it represents both the possessor and the thing possessed.

In the sentence, "That is his book," what is the predicate? "Book." What modifies "book"? "His," an adjective. What is "his"? It is a personal pronoun. Why is it not a possessive pronoun? Because it modifies the noun following it, and does not represent both the possessor and the thing possessed. It is a *possessive*, because it is used as an adjective; but it is not a *possessive pronoun* when used this way.

Write five sentences using possessive pronouns as **subjects**.

Model—*His* is a hard lot.

Write five sentences, using possessive pronouns as **predicates**.

Model—That desk is *mine*.

Analyze the following sentences, using these models.

MODELS

I. "Ours is an easy task."

This is a *sentence, declarative*.

Ours is the subject; **task**, the predicate; **is** is the copula. "Task" is modified by **an** and **easy**, both adjectives.

```
Ours | is : task
            | easy
            | an
```

II. "That factory is theirs."

This is a *sentence, declarative*.

Factory is the subject; **theirs**, the predicate; **is** is the copula. "Factory" is modified by **that**, an adjective.

III. "This land is our own."

This is a *sentence, declarative*.

Land is the subject; **our own**, the predicate. "Land" is modified by **this**, an adjective.

1. This book is hers. 2. Those apples are his. 3. Yours is a hard lesson. 4. Those marbles are mine. 5. This book is yours. 6. The evenings are our own. 7. The victory is ours.

Point out the **possessive pronouns** *in these sentences using this model.*

MODEL

"That book is mine."

Mine is a *pronoun, possessive*; it represents both the possessor and the thing possessed: it is equivalent to "my book."

Questions—What are possessive pronouns? Name some of them.

32. RELATIVE PRONOUNS

When we say, "A rich man owns that house," what element is the word "rich"? It is an adjective element. Why?

When we say, "A man who is rich, owns that house," what words do we use instead of "rich" to modify "man"? We use the words, "who is rich." What element do these words form? An adjective element. Why? Because they modify a noun.

Is the expression, "who is rich," a proposition? It is. Why? Because it has a subject and a predicate. What is the subject? "Who." Why? What is the predicate? "Rich." Why? What is the copula?

What part of speech is "who"? It is a pronoun. Why? It is a word used instead of a noun. Instead of what noun is it used? The noun *man*.

This sentence, then, contains two propositions: "A man owns that house," and "who is rich." The second proposition is an adjective element modifying the subject of the first. These propositions are called **clauses**.

The pronoun "who" is not only the subject of a proposition, but it also joins the modifying clause "who is rich" to the noun which it limits.

Those pronouns that represent preceding words or expressions, to which they join modifying clauses, are called *relative pronouns*.

A **relative pronoun** is a word used to represent a preceding word or expression, to which it joins a modifying clause. The relative pronouns are *who*, *which*, *what*, and *that*. *As* is also a relative after *such*, *many*, *same*, and some other words.

Rem.—The suffixes *ever*, *so*, and *soever*, are sometimes added to these pronouns; as, *whoever*, *whoso*, *whosoever*.

The word or expression represented by a relative pronoun, is called its **antecedent**.

Point out the relative pronouns in the following sentences, using the model below.

MODEL
"A man who is industrious will prosper."

Who is a *pronoun*, *relative*. It represents a preceding word, to which it joins a modifying clause. The word it represents is "man."

1. Tell me whom you saw. 2. Those who sow will reap. 3. He that hateth, dissembleth with his lips. 4. This is the house which my father bought.
5. I gave him all that I had. 6. Judge ye what I say. 7. He will do what is right. 8. A kind boy avoids doing whatever injures others. 9. Whoever studies will learn. 10. Whatever ye shall ask in my name, that will I do.

Substitute pronouns for the blanks in the following sentences.

1. Death lifts the veil ____ hides a brighter sphere. 2. ____ God, in ____ ____ trust. 3. The man ____ paid ____ the money was the cashier. 4. The message ____ ____ sent was received. 5. No one can tell _____ others may do. 6. _____ will do _____ is proper.

Questions—What are clauses? What is a relative pronoun? Name the pronouns in this class. What suffixes are sometimes added to relative pronouns? What is an antecedent?

33. THE RELATIVE CLAUSE

Clauses introduced by relative pronouns are called *relative clauses*.

A relative clause is a clause introduced by a relative pronoun.

Write five sentences, modifying their **subjects** *by relative clauses.*

Model—The boy who studies will learn.

Write five sentences, modifying their **objects** *by relative clauses.*

Model—I have lost the knife which you gave me.

Analyze the following sentences, using these models.

MODELS

I. "The fish which you caught is a trout."

This is a *sentence, declarative.*

Fish is the subject; **trout**, the predicate; **is**, the copula. "Fish" is modified by **the** and the clause **which you caught**, both adjective elements.

```
fish    |  is : trout
   The  '      |   a
   which you caught
```

II. "I like a horse that is gentle."

This is a *sentence, declarative.*

I is the subject; **like**, the predicate. "Like" is modified by **horse**, an objective element, which is modified by **a** and the clause **that is gentle**, both adjective elements.

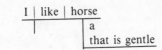

```
   I  |  like  |  horse
   |            |  a
                |  that is gentle
```

1. A very old man who is wealthy lives there. 2. I have a knife that has a white handle. 3. He who studies will learn. 4. You have many blessings which I cannot share. 5. Solomon, who was the son of David, built the temple. 6. He is a man who deserves respect. 7. The Lord chastens him whom he loves. 8. They who forsake the law praise the wicked.

*Use **adjectives** instead of **relative clauses** in the following sentences.*

1. I have an apple that is rotten. 2. A little boy who is lame came to our house yesterday. 3. I like people who are honest. 4. Will you buy me a knife that has four blades?

*Use **relative clauses** instead of **adjectives** in the following sentences.*

1. Industrious people always prosper. 2. There are many rich men in New York. 3. He has some counterfeit money. 4. A barking dog seldom bites. 5. The moldy paper was burned.

34. INTERROGATIVE PRONOUNS

In the sentences: "Who is that man?" "Which comes first?" "What is he?" what words are used instead of the answers to the questions? The words "who," "which," and "what."

Which and *what*, not used as modifiers, together with *who*, *whose*, and *whom*, when used in asking questions, are called *interrogative pronouns*.

The **interrogative pronouns** are *who*, *whose*, *whom*, *which*, and *what*, when used in asking questions.

Rem.—The words *which* and *what* are sometimes placed before nouns. They are then called *interrogative adjectives*.

Ex.—"Which road shall I take?" The word "which" is an interrogative adjective, modifying "road." "What noise is that?" The word "what" is an interrogative adjective, modifying "noise."

*Point out the **interrogative pronouns** in the following sentences, using this model.*

MODEL

"Who visited your school yesterday?"

Who is a *pronoun, interrogative*; it is used in asking a question.

1. What did he say? 2. Who wrote that letter? 3. Which trots the fastest? 4. Whom did you call? 5. Whose house was burned? 6. What can he mean? 7. Who has learned this lesson? 8. Who discovered America? 9. Who borrowed John's book? 10. Whose book is this?

*Point out the **nouns**, **adjectives**, **verbs**, **participles**, and **personal pronouns** in these sentences.*

Analyze the foregoing sentences, using this model.

MODEL

"Whom can you trust?"

This is a *sentence, interrogative.*

You is the subject; **can trust**, the predicate. "Can trust" is modified by **whom,** an object.

$$\text{You} \mid \text{can trust} \mid \text{whom?}$$

Questions—Define a relative clause. What is an interrogative pronoun? What words are used as interrogative pronouns? Which of these are sometimes used as interrogative objects?

35. INCORRECT LANGUAGE

Caution I—Do not use **him, me,** or **her** as the subject or the predicate of a sentence.

Ex.—1. Him and me were in the boat. 2. It was me. 3. Me and the doctor were there. 4. Him and you were tardy. 5. It is her. 6. You, and him, and me went swimming together.

Caution II—Do not use conversational English in formal writing. Formal: it is I, it is he, it is she, it is they (nominative pronoun after copula). Conversational: it's me, it's them (objective pronoun after copula).

Caution III—The pronoun **you** should precede **he, she,** or **they;** and **he, she,** or **they** should precede **I** or **we.**

Ex.—1. Aren't he and you brothers? 2. Don't they and you attend the same school? 3. I and you must study hard this forenoon. 4. We and he will stay in at recess. 5. We and you should go camping next vacation.

Caution IV—Do not use **which** to represent persons, or **who** or **whom** to represent animals or objects without life.

Ex.—1. The man which you saw is my father. 2. I love all which speak the truth. 3. Was that your dog who was killed? 4. I saw the man which was here yesterday.

THE ADVERB

36. ORAL LESSON

In the sentence, "Birds sing sweetly," does the word "sweetly" denote *what* the birds sing? It does not; it tells *how* they sing. Does it complete the meaning of the verb "sing," like an objective element? It does not; it modifies it in another way.

In the sentence, "Very large vessels were seen," what is modified by "very"? The word "large." What is "large"? It is an adjective.

In the sentence, "He rode quite fast," what word tells *how* he rode? The word "fast." What word tells *how fast* he rode? The word "quite."

Words used in this manner are called *adverbs*.

An **adverb** is a word used to modify a verb, an adjective, a participle, or another adverb.

*Point out the **adverbs** in the following sentences, using this model.*

MODEL

"The wind blew furiously."

Furiously is an *adverb*; it is used to modify a verb.

1. That vessel sails slowly. 2. He built a house there. 3. Mike is usually early. 4. Those mountains are very high. 5. We were agreeably surprised. 6. I will shortly return. 7. You will never see him again. 8. I would gladly forgive you. 9. So said Tom. 10. He afterwards escaped.

*Point out the **nouns, verbs, pronouns,** and **adjectives** in these sentences.*

*Point out the **adverbs** in your reading lesson.*

*Write seven sentences, modifying their **predicates** by adverbs.*

Model—We should walk *quietly*.

*Write seven sentences, modifying their **subjects** by adjectives and these adjectives by adverbs.*

Model—*Very* loud reports were heard.

*Write seven sentences, modifying their **predicates** by adverbs and those adverbs by other adverbs.*

Model—He walks *quite* slowly.

37. THE ADVERBIAL ELEMENT

A word or group of words used like an adverb—that is, used to modify a verb, an adjective, a participle, or an adverb—is called an *adverbial element*.

An **adverbial element** is a word or group of words used to modify a verb, an adjective, a participle, or an adverb. The *adverbial element* may be an ordinary adverb, as *carefully*; a pronoun, as *ours*; a clause or phrase; or even many words generally used as other parts of speech.

Adverbial element is the broad, general term used in this text to identify all words and word groups used as adverbs, to point out their *function* in a specific sentence. Often the terms *adverb* and *adverbial element* are nearly synonymous, though the former speaks of *form* of words and the latter refers to their *function* in sentences.

In the strictest sense, no word is an *adverb* until it is so used, though words ending in *ly* are nearly always used only as *adverbial elements*.

Analyze the sentences in the preceding section, using these models.

MODELS

I. "Our house is very small."

This is a *sentence, declarative.*

House is the subject; **small**, the predicate; **is**, the copula. "House" is modified by **our** and **small**, adjective elements; "small," by **very**, an adverbial element.

```
house  | is : small
  | Our|       | very
```

II. "We should study our lessons carefully."

This is a *sentence, declarative.*

We is the subject; **should study**, the predicate. "Should study" is modified by **lessons**, an object/objective element, and by **carefully**, an adverb/adverbial element. "Lessons" is modified by **our**, an adjective/adjective element.

```
We | should study | lessons
   |    | carefully |    | our
```

Questions—What is an adverb? What do adverbs usually denote? What is an adverbial element?

38. THE ADVERBIAL CLAUSE

In the sentence, "Flowers bloom when spring comes," what group of words tells when flowers bloom? The group "when spring comes." What element is this group? It is an adverbial element. Why? Because it modifies the verb "bloom."

Is this group a proposition? It is. Why? Because it contains a subject and a predicate. What is the subject? "Spring." Why? What is the predicate?

"Comes." Why? The group is called an *adverbial clause*, because it contains a subject and a predicate, and is used as an adverbial element.

An **adverbial clause** is a clause used as an adverbial element.

Adverbial clauses begin with subordinating conjunctions such as *when, where, while, because, if, after, as, although, though*, and a large number of other words.

Point out the adverbial clauses in the following sentences.

1. I left the spade where I found it. 2. John was listening while you were talking. 3. The bear growled when he saw the hunter. 4. I cannot go before my father returns. 5. Henry will play with you if you desire it. 6. We traveled slowly because we wished to see the country. 7. I can go now for my task is finished.

Analyze the above sentences, using the following model.

MODEL

"He trembles when it thunders."

This is a *sentence, declarative.*

He is the subject; **trembles**, the predicate. "Trembles" is modified by the clause **when it thunders**, an adverbial element.

```
He | trembles
   |        | when it thunders
```

Questions—What is an adverbial clause? With what words do adverbial clauses begin?

Rem.—A special group of adverbs are called *negatives*. These include *no, never*, and *not*, and the prefixes *non* and *un*, which are related to the pronoun *none* and are sometimes used as adjectives.

These negatives are usually used to modify verbs or adjectives in sentences such as, "I am *never* going" ("never" modifies "am going"); "That is *no* good" ("no" modifies the adjective "good"). They are also found in contractions such as, "*Don't* do it" ("n-t" modifies the verb, "do").

Negative adjectives may sometimes be repeated for emphasis; as "No, I am *not* going."

39. INCORRECT LANGUAGE

Caution I—Do not use such double negatives as, **I don't see nothing, Don't tell nobody**, etc., because this makes a positive—a contradiction. "I *don't* see *nothing*" means "I *do* see *something*."

Ex.—1. I don't want nothing today. 2. Don't tell nobody nothing about it. 3. We didn't catch no fish. 4. John don't feel no better than he did yesterday.

Caution II—Do not use **adjectives** as **adverbs**.

Ex.—1. Drive careful in traffic. 2. Doesn't Mary dress neat? 3. Brad speaks very distinct. 4. Tom spells exceptional. 5. Always speak distinct.

Caution III—Do not use **adverbs** as **adjectives**.

Ex.—1. I felt sickly yesterday. 2. This flower smells sweetly. 3. Stand as nearly to me as you can. 4. The countryside looks beautifully after a shower. 5. Things look somewhat more favorably this morning. 6. The doctor said that his patient felt more comfortably.

40. COMPOSITION

Read the following description three or four times, then reproduce it from memory. After your teacher has seen your work on "The Lion," write a one-page story of your own, describing another beast. Use specific details, such as you may find in an encyclopedia or perhaps have observed at a zoo.

THE LION

A full grown lion is nearly nine feet in length, and between four and five feet in height. The female, or lioness, is about three fourths as large as the male. The body of the lion is covered with hair of a tawny color. The male has a long and thick mane, which he can stand up when he desires. A lioness has no mane.

The lion lives entirely upon the flesh of other animals. He usually crouches in a thicket and watches until some animal passes within fifteen or twenty feet of him. Then he leaps upon it and generally seizes it at the first bound. Should he happen to miss his object, he returns to his hiding place, with a measured step, where he waits for another opportunity.

He most frequently hides near a spring or a river so he may seize the animals which come there to quench their thirst. A lion rarely attacks men, unless it is wounded or driven by hunger.

THE PREPOSITION

41. ORAL LESSON

In the sentence, "A man of wealth rode by our house," what does the group of words "of wealth" modify? It modifies the noun "man." What element is it? It is an adjective element. Why? Because it modifies a noun.

What does the group of words "by our house" modify? It modifies the verb "rode": it tells *where* he rode. What element is it? It is an adverbial element. Why? Because it modifies a verb.

The word "of" connects the noun "wealth" to the noun "man." The word "by" connects the noun "house" with the verb "rode." They are said to show the *relations* between the words which they connect, and are called *prepositions*. The nouns which follow them are called their **objects**.

A **preposition** is a word used to show the relation between its object and some other word.

LIST OF THE PRINCIPAL PREPOSITIONS

A = *at*, *on*, or *in*	As to	Except	Till, until
Aboard	At	For	Through
About	Before	From	Throughout
Above	Behind	In, into	To
According to	Beside, besides	Of	Toward
Across	Beneath	Off	Towards
After	Between	On	Under
Against	Beyond	Outside	Unto
Along	But	Over	Up
Amid, amidst	By	Past	Upon
Among, amongst	Down	Round	With
Around	During	Since	Within

Point out the **prepositions** *in the following sentences, using this model.*

MODEL

"He came from France to America."

From is a *preposition*; it shows the relation between its object and some other word. It shows the relation between "France" and "came." **To** is a *preposition*; it shows the relation between "America" and "came."

1. The old man was often in want of the necessities of life. 2. The boy went through the gate into the garden. 3. He was not, at that time, in the city. 4. He drove over the bridge into the city. 5. He went to the doctor for advice. 6. The path brought them to the end of the wood. 7. She turned to the old man with a lovely smile upon her face. 8. The light came through the stained glass windows of the old church.

Point out the **nouns, verbs, adjectives,** *and* **pronouns** *in these sentences.*

Questions—What is a preposition? What is the object of a preposition? Name the principal prepositions.

42. THE PHRASE

I

1. A group of words consisting of a preposition and its object is called a **phrase**.

Phrases are most commonly used as adjective or adverbial elements.

Analyze the following sentences, using this model.

MODEL

"Habits of industry will lead to prosperity."

This is a *sentence, declarative.*

Habits is the subject; **will lead**, the predicate. "Habits" is modified by the phrase **of industry**, an adjective element; "will lead" is modified by the phrase **to prosperity**, an adverbial element.

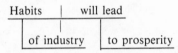

1. Light moves in straight lines. 2. They went aboard the ship. 3. I differ from you on that point. 4. The two thieves divided the money between them. 5. The ship was driven upon the rocks.

6. Our sincerest laughter is fraught with some pain. 7. The young lambs are bleating in the meadows. 8. They came to the country of the free. 9. I will divide this farm among my three sons. 10. Man goeth to his long home. 11. The sleep of a laboring man is sweet.

*Substitute **single words or clauses** for the **phrases** in the following sentences.*

Models—I. "Henry studies his lessons with care" = "Henry studies his lessons carefully." II. "Ice forms in cold weather" = "Ice forms when the weather is cold."

1. The sailors weighed anchor at sunrise. 2. The enraged lion struggled in vain. 3. Flowers bloom in the spring. 4. Some seed fell on stony ground. 5. The face of the poor boy was disfigured. 6. I have written this letter in haste.

II

In the sentence, "To play is pleasant," "to play" is the subject. Why? It is that of which something is affirmed. It is a form of the verb "play." It expresses action, but does not affirm it. For this reason, it is called an *infinitive* or an *infinitive phrase.*

2. An **infinitive** is a form of the verb used to express action without affirming it.

Rem.—The word "to" is usually placed before the verb, and is called the sign of the infinitive. The two parts should not be separated in analyzing or parsing.

An infinitive may be the subject or the predicate of a sentence or clause; or an adjective, objective, or adverbial element.

Analyze the following sentences, using these models.

MODELS

I. "To love is to obey."

This is a *sentence, declarative.*
To love is the subject; **to obey**, the predicate; **is**, the copula.

```
To love | is : to obey
         |
```

II. "The lawyer went to his office to write a letter."

This is a *sentence, declarative.*
Lawyer is the subject; **went**, the predicate. "Lawyer" is modified by **the**, an adjective; "went," by the phrases **to his office** and **to write a letter**, both adverbial elements. "Office" is modified by **his**, an adjective element; "to write," by **letter**, an object, which is modified by **a**, an adjective.

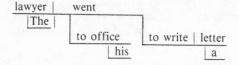

1. To lie is wicked. 2. He wants to go to the city. 3. To doubt the promise of a true friend is a sin. 4. John studies to learn. 5. My sister wishes to remain here. 6. Are you ready to recite your lesson? 7. Ambitious boys like to work hard. 8. To teach the young is a pleasant task.

III

The meaning of a sentence may often be changed by changing the position of the single words, phrases, and clauses of which it is composed.

In the sentence, "Only John studies algebra," "only" modifies "John." He is the only person that studies algebra. In the sentence, "John studies algebra only," "only" modifies "algebra." It is the only subject that John studies.

In the sentence, "A watch was found yesterday by a student with steel hands," the phrase "with steel hands" modifies "student"; but in the sentence, "A watch with steel hands was found yesterday by a student," the phrase "with steel hands" modifies "watch." In the first sentence, the *student* has steel hands; in the second, the *watch*.

In the sentence, "He needs no glasses who cannot see," the clause "who cannot see" is not intended to be used as a modifier of "glasses," but of the word "he." It should be placed between "he" and "needs."

Rule—Words, phrases, and clauses, used as modifiers, should be placed as near the modified words as possible.

Locate the phrases and clauses properly in these sentences.

1. The sled was bought by a boy going to school for a dollar. 2. Wanted—a horse by an English gentleman sixteen hands high. 3. Look at those two men fishing with sunburnt faces. 4. The book was dropped by a careless boy on my head. 5. I saw a dog bite a man with long ears and a white spot on his face. 6. Mr. Otis needs a surgeon who has broken his arm. 7. A silver fruit knife was found by a child which has a broken handle.

Questions—What is a phrase? An infinitive? Give the rule for the placing of modifying words, phrases, and clauses.

THE CONJUNCTION

43. ORAL LESSON

In the sentence, "Ellen and Mary study botany," what two words are used as the subject? "Ellen" and "Mary." Why? Because something is affirmed of them: both Ellen and Mary study botany. What word connects the words "Ellen" and "Mary"? The word "and."

In the sentence, "Ellen or Mary studies botany," what two words are used as the subject? "Ellen" and "Mary." Are both represented as studying botany? They are not: if Ellen studies botany, Mary does not. What word connects the words "Ellen" and "Mary"? The word "or."

In the statement, "Ellen will study botany, if Mary studies algebra," how many clauses are there? There are two: "Ellen will study botany," and "Mary studies algebra." What word is used to connect these two clauses? The word "if."

The words "and," "or," "if," and all other words used merely to join words or groups of words, are called *conjunctions*.

A **conjunction** is a word used to connect words, phrases, clauses, and members.

Conjunctions merely *connect* words, phrases, clauses, and members; they do not express *relations*, like prepositions.

Point out the **conjunctions** *in the following sentences, using this model.*

MODEL

"Mark and Andy will improve, if they study."

And is a *conjunction*; it is a word used to connect words: it connects "Mark" and "Andy." **If** is a *conjunction*; it connects the clauses, "Mark and Andy will improve" and "they study."

1. We moved along silently and cautiously. 2. I consent to the Constitution because it protects our rights. 3. He heaped up great riches but passed his time miserably. 4. He is both learned and wise. 5. I shall not go if it rains. 6. They submit, since they cannot conquer. 7. He has many faults; still he is very popular. 8. Debbie or Susan will remain at home.

Questions—What is a conjunction? What is the difference between a conjunction and a preposition?

44. COMPOUND ELEMENTS

"Jim and Sam are kind, honest, and faithful." In this sentence, "Jim" and "Sam" are the *parts* of what is called a *compound subject*; "kind," "honest," and "faithful," are the *parts* of a *compound predicate*.

Two or more similar parts of a proposition, connected by conjunctions, form a *compound element*.

A **compound element** consists of two or more similar parts of the same proposition clause connected by conjunctions.

Rem. 1—The conjunctions may be expressed or understood.
Any element of a proposition may be compound.

Directions for Writing—When a compound element consists of **more than** two parts:
I. Place a comma after each part except the last.
II. Use the conjunction between the last two parts only.

When a compound element consists of only two parts:
I. Connect them by a conjunction.
II. Or omit the conjunction and use a comma in its stead.

Rem. 2—When it is the intention of the writer to make the parts emphatic, the conjunction and the comma may both be used between any two of them.

*Write five sentences, each containing a **compound subject**.*

Model—Ellen and Lucy are my sisters.

*Write five sentences, each containing a **compound predicate**.*

Model—We run, jump, and play ball at recess.

*Write five sentences, each containing a **compound object**.*

Model—My father owns a farm and a factory.

*Write five sentences, each containing a **compound adjective**.*

Model—Shep is a large, black, and gentle dog.

*Write five sentences, each containing a **compound adverb**.*

Model—We stopped then and there.

Analyze the following sentences, using these models.

MODELS

I. "Bill and Henry study algebra."

This is a *sentence, declarative*.
Bill and Henry is the compound subject; **study**, the predicate. "Study" is modified by **algebra**, an object.

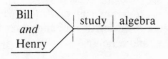

II. "Mr. Edson buys and sells butter and eggs."

This is a *sentence, declarative*.
Mr. Edson is the subject; **buys and sells**, the compound predicate, which is modified by **butter and eggs**, a compound object.

III. "The two boys slipped along silently and cautiously."

This is a *sentence, declarative.*

Boys is the subject; **slipped**, the predicate. "Boys" is modified by **the** and **two**, adjectives; "slipped," by **along**, an adverb, and by **silently and cautiously**, a compound **adverb**.

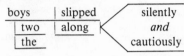

1. Exercise and temperance strengthen the soul. 2. Mr. Mann owns and cultivates a large and valuable farm. 3. Two and two are four. 4. Duty and holiness forbid harmful and wicked habits. 5. Forty pupils study arithmetic, grammar, and geography. 6. The weary soldiers fought bravely and successfully.

Questions—What is a compound element? Give directions for writing a compound element consisting of more than two parts. Of two parts only.

45. SIMPLE SENTENCES

"Wheat is a grain." This sentence consists of a single proposition. It is called a *simple sentence.*

A **simple sentence** consists of a single proposition.

In the sentences, "I see a dog," "I see a boy," "I see a tree," "I see a house," "I see" is a part common to all of them. We may combine these, and form a single sentence, by using this common part only once; thus, "I see a dog, a boy, a tree, and a house."

*Combine the sentences in the following paragraphs into **single sentences**.*

1. I found a book. I found a pencil. I found a pen. I found a knife.

2. Apple trees grow vigorously. Apples grow in our orchard.

3. John walked to the lake. John walked over the hill. John walked rapidly.

4. The horse was old. The horse was lame. The horse was blind.

5. The wind blew fiercely. The wind blew last night. The wind blew from the north.

6. Uncle William gave me a new book. Uncle William loaned me his shotgun. Uncle William bought a sled for my brother.

Questions—What is a simple sentence? How may several sentences be combined so as to form a single sentence?

46. COMPOUND SENTENCES

"Wheat grows in the field, and men reap it." This sentence consists of two propositions, each of which will make complete sense when standing alone. It is called a *compound sentence*.

1. **A compound sentence** consists of two or more connected sentences, each of which will make complete sense when standing alone.

Rem.—The sentences of which a compound sentence is composed, are called *independent clauses*.

In the sentence, "Exercise strengthens the soul, and temperance strengthens the soul," "exercise" and "temperance" are parts not common to the two clauses. The sentence may be changed to a simple one by uniting these, and using the common parts but once; thus, "Exercise and temperance strengthen the soul."

2. A compound sentence containing common parts, may be changed to a simple one by uniting the parts not common to all its clauses, and using the common parts but once.

Write five **compound sentences**, *each containing two clauses.*

Change the following compound sentences to simple ones.

1. Behold my mother and behold my brethren. 2. I saw a man in a boat and I saw a boy in the water. 3. Washington was a warrior and Washington was a statesman. 4. The man you saw was sick, or he was in trouble. 5. The river was swift, and it was very deep.

Analyze the following sentences, using this model.

MODEL

"The heavens declare the glory of God, and the firmament showeth his handiwork" *(Psalm 19:1).*

This is a *sentence, compound.* "The heavens declare the glory of God" is the first independent clause; "the firmament showeth his handiwork," the second independent clause; "and" is the connective.

Heavens is the subject of the first independent clause; **declare**, the predicate. "Heavens" is modified by **the**, an adjective; "declare," by **glory**, an object, which is modified by **the** and the phrase **of God**, adjective elements.

Firmament is the subject of the second clause; **showeth**, the predicate. "Firmament" is modified by **the**, an adjective; "showeth," by **handiwork**, an object which is modified by **his**, an adjective.

```
heavens | declare | glory
   | The |        | the | of God
```

and

```
firmament | showeth | handiwork
   | the    |         | his
```

1. Talent is something, but tact is everything. 2. Art is long, and time is fleeting. 3. Lead us not into temptation, but deliver us from evil. 4. The gathering clouds threatened an approaching storm, and the deep darkness of the night soon enveloped them. 5. The stores were closed and the hum of business was hushed. 6. Every eye was filled with tears, and, for a moment, all were silent. 7. You may stay here with me, or we will go to church with Susan.

Questions—What is a compound sentence? What are its members? How can a compound sentence containing common parts, be changed to a simple sentence?

47. COMPLEX SENTENCES

I

A *complex sentence* must contain an *independent*, *principle clause*, and one or more *subordinate clauses*. A clause must contain a subject and a predicate.

1. A **complex sentence** has a principle clause and one or more subordinate clauses.

In the complex sentence, "I know where gold is found," the first clause, "I know," makes complete sense when standing alone. It is therefore called the *principal clause*.

2. A **principal clause** is one which makes complete sense when separated from the rest of the sentence.

The second clause, "where gold is found," does not make complete sense when standing alone, and it is therefore called a *subordinate clause*.

3. A **subordinate clause** has a subject and predicate, but it does not make complete sense when separated from the rest of the sentence.

Clauses may also be divided into the following five classes: *subject, predicate, objective, adjective,* and *adverbial.*

Rem.—Some complex sentences are composed of many clauses. Each clause should be analyzed in the order indicated by its position.

MODELS FOR COMPLETE ANALYSIS

I. "He that hateth, dissembleth with his lips."

This is a *sentence, declarative, complex*; it is composed of a principal clause and a subordinate clause. "He dissembleth with his lips" is the principal clause; "that hateth," the subordinate clause.

He is the subject of the principal clause; **dissembleth,** the predicate. "He" is modified by the clause **that hateth,** an adjective element, of which **that** is the subject, and **hateth,** the predicate. "Dissembleth" is modified by the phrase **with his lips,** an adverbial element; "lips," by **his,** an adjective.

```
He                    |  dissembleth
        | that | hateth  |      | with lips
        |                        |   his
```

II. "That he is very sick, is evident."

This is a *sentence, declarative, complex*; its subject is a clause. **That he is very sick** is the subject; **evident,** the predicate; **is,** the copula. **He** is the subject of the subject clause; **sick,** the predicate; **is,** the copula. "Sick" is modified by **very,** an adverb. **That** is a conjunction used to introduce the subject clause.

```
(That) he | is : sick
          |        | very | is : evident
          |
```

III. "He never denied that the letter was lost."

This is a *sentence, declarative, complex*. "He never denied" is the principal clause; "the letter was lost," the subordinate clause. "That" is the connective.

He is the subject of the principal clause; **denied**, the predicate, which is modified by **never**, an adverb, and by the clause **that the letter was lost**, an objective element. **Letter** is the subject of the subordinate clause; **was lost**, the predicate. "Letter" is modified by **the**, an adjective. **That** is a connective joining the clause "the letter was lost" to "denied."

```
                         | (that) letter | was lost
        He | denied                 | the |
               | never
```

IV. "He builds a palace of ice where the torrents fall."

This is a *sentence, declarative, complex*. "He builds a palace of ice" is the principal clause; "the torrents fall," the subordinate clause. "Where" is the connective.

He is the subject of the principal clause; **builds**, the predicate, which is modified by **palace**, an object, and by the clause **where the torrents fall**, an adverbial element. "Palace" is modified by **a** and the phrase **of ice**, adjective elements; "torrents," by **the**, an adjective; "fall," by **where**, an adverb.

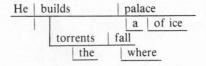

1. He that flatters, deceives his neighbor. 2. The boy that you saw, is my younger brother. 3. He was frightened when he first saw a lion. 4. I cannot study where pupils make so much noise. 5. I would pay you if I had the money. 6. That he will succeed is certain. 7. The messenger reported that the brave general was dead. 8. Nature never did betray the heart that loved her.

10. The poor too often turn away, unheard,
From hearts that shut against them, with a sound
That shall be heard in heaven.—*Longfellow.*

*Write five sentences, using clauses as **subjects**.*

Model—"Haste makes waste" is a true saying.

*Write five sentences, using clauses as **objects**.*

Model—We know that the earth is round.

*Write five sentences, using clauses as **adjective elements**.*

Model—The report that he is insane is unfounded.

*Write five sentences, using clauses as **adverbial elements**.*

Model—Our teacher is delighted when we are studious.

Analyze the sentences you have written.

II

4. For simplicity, complex sentences may often be reduced to simple sentences by using single words or phrases, instead of subordinate propositions, as modifiers.

Reduce the following complex sentences to simple sentences.

Models—I. "A man who is wealthy, lives there" = "A man of wealth lives there," or, "A wealthy man lives there."
II. "We started when the sun rose" = "We started at sunrise."

1. A pupil who is studious will learn rapidly. 2. Men who are honest, are respected. 3. A boy when he is at play is happy. 4. An accident that was unavoidable occurred at the factory this morning. 5. Franklin, who was a philosopher, was an American. 6. One soldier was not present when the roll was called. 7. They weighed anchor when the tide turned. 8. My brother has gone to the city that he may find employment.

5. For clarity simple sentences may occasionally need to be enlarged to complex sentences by using subordinate propositions, instead of single words or phrases, as modifiers.

Enlarge the following simple sentences.

Ex.—"None think the great unhappy but the great" = "None think that the great are unhappy but the great."

Rem.—Always *prefer* the simple sentence modified by single words or short phrases to the complex or compound sentence. Needless words make writing dull, and bore readers.

Enlarge simple sentences to complex ones only when the infinitive or prepositional phrase modifier is awkward or unclear. Alexander Pope's famous line, "To err is human; to forgive, divine" would never have been remembered—for more than 200 years—had he written, "Making an error is human, but forgiveness is that which is divine."

Questions—What is a complex sentence? A principal clause? A subordinate clause? Into what five classes may clauses be divided? How may complex sentences be reduced? How may simple sentences sometimes be enlarged?

THE INTERJECTION

48. ORAL LESSON

"Hurrah! We have found him."

Is this a sentence? It is. What is the subject? The pronoun "we." What is the predicate? "Have found." What modifies the predicate? The pronoun "him," an object.

What does the word "hurrah" denote? It denotes that the speaker or writer is highly pleased. Does it affirm or deny anything? It does not: it simply implies a feeling or emotion of pleasure.

There are words, also, used to denote sorrow, grief, surprise, disgust, pity, hatred, etc.

All such words are called *interjections*.

An **interjection** is a word used to denote some sudden or strong emotion.

Rem.—Interjections usually, but not always, require an exclamation point [!] after them.

Point out the interjections in each of the following sentences, using this model.

MODEL

"Shh! They are coming."

Shh is an *interjection*; it denotes some sudden emotion.

1. Listen! The clock strikes one. 2. Phooey! I knew that yesterday. 3. Alas! We shall see him no more. 4. Aye, he is every inch a king. 5. Hark, hark! The lark at heaven's gate sings. 6. Ouch! That hurts. 7. Help! Someone throw that man a rope.

Point out all the parts of speech in the above sentences.

Questions—What is an interjection? What should usually be placed after an interjection?

PART II

SYNTAX—COMPOSITION

49. PROPERTIES OF THE NOUN

To the noun belong *gender*, *person*, *number*, and *case*. These are called its **properties**.

50. GENDER

Objects are either male or female; as, *boy*, *girl*; or neither male nor female; as, *apple*. Their names, therefore may be classified with regard to *sex*. This distinction is called *gender*.

1. **Gender** is a distinction of nouns or pronouns with regard to sex.

2. There are four genders: *masculine*, *feminine*, *common*, and *neuter*.

3. The **masculine gender** denotes males; as, *boy*, *man*.

4. The **feminine gender** denotes females; as, *girl*, *woman*.

Some words, as *children*, *parent*, etc., are used to denote *either* males or females. The gender of such words is said to be *common*.

5. The **common gender** denotes either males or females; as, *parent*.

6. The **neuter gender** denotes neither males nor females; as, *house*.

7. There are three ways of distinguishing the masculine and feminine genders:

1. *By using different words*; as, father, mother; brother, sister; boy, girl; gentleman, lady; Mr., Mrs.; drake, duck; hart, roe; Charles, Caroline; (*Charles* and *Caroline* are variant spellings of the same name).

2. *By different terminations*; as, actor, actress; executor, executrix; hero, heroine.

3. *By joining some distinguishing word*; as, man-servant, maid-servant; he-bear, she-bear; landlord, landlady; merman, mermaid.

*Tell the **gender** of the following nouns.*

Cart	Duke	Father	Nephew	Countess
Poet	Susan	Joseph	Butcher	President
Aunt	Baker	Madam	Empress	Administratrix

*Give the corresponding **masculine** or **feminine** for the following nouns.*

King	Uncle	Francis	Pauline	Miss Jones
Niece	Widow	Brother	Sorcerer	Grandfather
Count	Female	Prophet	Mediator	Hen

*Write five sentences, using **masculine** nouns as subjects.*

Model—*John* left his book on my desk.

*Write five sentences, using **feminine** nouns as objects.*

Model—The teacher sent my *sister* home at recess.

*Write six sentences, using nouns in the **common** or **neuter** gender as subjects or objects.*

Model—A *dog* frightened me this morning.

*Tell the **gender** of all the nouns in your reading lesson.*

Questions—What belong to nouns? What is gender? How many genders are there? What is the masculine gender? The feminine gender? The common gender? The neuter gender? How many ways are there of distinguishing the masculine and feminine genders? Give them.

51. PERSON

1. **Person** is that property of a noun or pronoun which distinguishes the speaker, the person spoken to, and the person or object spoken of.

2. There are three persons, *first*, *second*, and *third*. (See Section 30.)

*Tell the **person** of the nouns and pronouns in the following sentences.*

1. My lesson is learned. 2. Have you seen our old friend lately? 3. Ellen, tell your sister to come home. 4. I saw him on New Year's Eve. 5. Your horse is in our barn, Mr. Eckel. 6. He left home early in the morning.

*Write five sentences, using nouns or pronouns of the **first person** as subjects, predicates, or objects.*

Model—*We* are students. *I* defended *myself.*

*Write five sentences, using nouns or pronouns of the **second person** as subjects or objects.*

Model—*You* may be excused. I envy *you.*

*Write five sentences, using nouns or pronouns of the **third person** as subjects, predicates, or objects.*

Models—Studious *pupils* learn long *lessons* easily. *They* left their *homes* in *sorrow.*

Questions—What is person? How many persons are there? Define them.

52. NUMBER

1. **Number** is that property of a noun or pronoun which distinguishes one from more than one.

2. There are two numbers, *singular* and *plural*. (See Section 8.)

53. FORMATION OF THE PLURAL

1. Nouns whose last sound will unite with *s*, form their plurals by adding *s* only to the singular; as, book, *books*; boy, *boys*; desk, *desks*.

2. Nouns whose last sound will not unite with *s*, form their plurals by adding *es* to the singular; as, bush, *bushes*; box, *boxes*.

3. Nouns ending in *y* preceded by a consonant, change *y* into *i*, and add *es*; as, mercy, *mercies*.

4. Some nouns ending in *f* or *fe* change these endings into *ves*; as, knife, *knives*.

5. Most nouns ending in *o*, preceded by a consonant, add *es*; as, cargo, *cargoes*; potato, *potatoes*.

6. Nouns ending in *o*, preceded by a vowel, add *s* ; as, folio, *folios*.

7. Letters, figures, marks, and signs add *'s*; as, *p's* and *q's*; *9's* and *11's*; the **'s*; the *&'s* and *$'s*.

8. Proper nouns usually add *s* only in forming their plurals; as, Mary, *Marys*; Sarah, *Sarahs*; Nero, *Neros*. The forms *Maries*, *Neroes*, etc., are sometimes used.

9. Most nouns from foreign languages change *us* to *i*; *um* and *on* to *a*; *is* to *es* or *ides*; *a* to *oe* or *ata*; and *x* to *ces* or *ices*; as, calculus, *calculi*; emporium, *emporia*; phenomenon, *phenomena*; thesis, *theses*.

10. Some nouns form their plurals irregularly, as, man, *men*; ox, *oxen*; mouse, *mice*.

11. A few nouns are alike in both numbers; as, *sheep*, *deer*, *trout*, *yoke*, *hose* (garment), *vermin*, and others.

12. In compound words, the part described by the rest is generally pluralized; as, *brothers*-in-law, *courts*-martial, ox-*carts*.

13. Nouns ending in *ful* or *full*, form their plurals by adding *s* to the singular; as, *handfuls*, *mouthfuls*.

Write the **plurals** *of the following words, letters, and signs.*

Calf	Clam	Truth	A, b, c	Analysis
Tax	Dick	Tooth	Armful	Mischief
+, -	Folly	Reply	Charles	Creature
Hoe	Rake	Horse	Salmon	Chimney
Turf	Child	Radix	Woman	Embargo
Vase	Glory	Studio	Wife	Momentum
Plow	Life	Cameo	Wrench	Wagon load

Write the **singular** *of the following nouns.*

Feet	Geese	Errata	Heroes	Ellipses
Mice	Folios	Rubies	Badges	Beauties
Oxen	Pennies	Loaves	Judges	Children
Genii	Strata	Horses	Valleys	Monkeys

Tell the **number** *of all the nouns in your reading lesson.*

Questions—What is number? How many numbers are there? What is the singular number? The plural number? Repeat the rules for the formation of the plural.

54. CASE

"The sun is shining": here "sun" is used as the subject of a proposition. "Every star is a sun": here "sun" is used as the predicate. "The sun's rays are warm": here "sun" is used as an adjective element, modifying "rays." "We saw the sun at noon": here "sun" is used as an objective element, modifying "saw." "Dear is thy light, O sun!" here "sun" is used absolutely—*i.e.*, it is *absolved* or separated from any grammatical connection with the rest of the sentence.

In no two of these sentences has the word "sun" the same relation to the other words.

These different relations are called *cases*.

1. **Case** is the relation of a noun or a pronoun to other words.

Rem.—The term *case* is also applied to the *form* of a noun or a pronoun used independently or as a part of a sentence.

2. There are four cases: *nominative, possessive, objective,* and *absolute,* or *nominative absolute.*

3. The **nominative case** is the use of a noun or pronoun as the subject or the predicate of a proposition; as, *Boys* skate; *Horses* are *animals.*

4. The **possessive case** is the use of a noun or pronoun to denote ownership, authorship, origin, or kind; as, *John's* hat, *Ray's* Algebra, the *sun's* rays, *men's* clothing.

Note—For rules for forming the possessive case, see Section 29, parts II and III.

5. The **objective case** is the use of a noun or pronoun as the object of a transitive verb in the active voice, or of a preposition; as, "Indians hunt *buffaloes,*" "They ran over the *bridge,*" "John threw a *ball* across the *diamond.*"

6. The **absolute,** or **nominative absolute, case** is the use of a noun or pronoun independent of any governing word; as, "Oh, my *son!*" "*Soldiers,* attention!" "*Washington Irving.*"

Rem.—A noun may be in the absolute case:

1. *By direct address*; as, "*James,* bring me a book."
2. *By exclamation*; as, "Oh, my *daughter!*"
3. *By redundancy*; *i.e.,* by placing it before a sentence in which an affirmation is made concerning it; as, "Your *fathers,* where are they?"
4. *With a participle*; as, "The *sun* being risen."
5. *By position*; *i.e.,* by using it as the heading of a chapter, as the superscription to a letter, etc.; as, "*The Noun,*" "*M. F. Jones.*"

7. A noun limiting the meaning of another noun denoting the same person or thing, is, by **apposition,** in the same case; as, "Washington the *general* became Washington the *statesman.*" "General" and "statesman" are both *nominative case,* since "Washington" in both positions is *nominative.*

55. DECLENSION

The **declension** of a noun is its variation to denote number and case.

Rem.—The absolute case always has the same form as the nominative. The objective case also has the same form as the nominative, except for certain pronouns.

EXAMPLE

	Singular	Plural		Singular	Plural
Nom.	Fly	Flies	*Nom.*	Goodness	_____
Poss.	Fly's	Flies'	*Poss.*	Goodness'	_____
Obj.	Fly	Flies	*Obj.*	Goodness	_____

Questions—What is case? How many cases are there? What is the nominative case? The possessive case? The objective case? The absolute case? How is the possessive case singular formed? The possessive case plural? In how many ways may a noun be in the absolute case? Give examples.

What is declension? Decline "boy," "girl," "farmer."

56. PARSING

Parsing consists (1) In naming the part of speech; (2) In telling its properties; (3) In pointing out its relations to other words; (4) In giving the rule for its construction.

57. ORDER OF PARSING

1. A noun, and why? 2. Common or proper, and why? 3. Gender, and why? 4. Person, and why? 5. Number, and why? 6. Case, and why? 7. Rule for construction.

58. MODELS FOR PARSING

I. "Wheat is a cereal."

Wheat is a *noun*; it is a name: *common*; it can be applied to any one of a kind or class: *neuter gender*; it denotes neither males nor females: *third person*; it is spoken of: *singular number*; it denotes but one: *nominative case*; it is used as the subject of the proposition. Rule I. "A noun or pronoun used as the subject of a proposition is in the nominative case."

Cereal is a *noun*; *common*; *neuter*; *third person*; *singular number*; *nominative case*; it is used as the predicate of the proposition. Rule II. "A noun or pronoun used as the predicate of a proposition is in the nominative case."

II. "Henry's uncle, the sheriff, was wounded."

Henry's is a *noun*; *proper*; it is the name of a particular person: *masculine gender*; it denotes a male: *third person*; *singular number*; *possessive case*;

it denotes possession, and modifies "uncle." Rule III. "A noun or pronoun used to limit the meaning of a noun denoting a different person or thing is in the possessive case."

Sheriff is a *noun*; *common*; *masculine gender*; *third person*; *singular number*; *nominative case*, in apposition with "uncle," which it modifies. Rule IV. "A noun or pronoun used to limit the meaning of a noun or pronoun by denoting the same person, place, or thing is in the same case."

III. "Sam, study your lesson with care."

Sam is a *noun*; *proper*; *masculine gender*; *second person*; it denotes the person addressed; *singular number*; it denotes only one: *absolute case*; it is used independently. Rule V. "A noun or pronoun used independently is in the absolute case."

Lesson is a *noun*; *common*; *neuter gender*; *third person*; *singular number*; *objective case*; it is the object of the verb "study." Rule VI. "The object of a transitive verb in the active voice, or of its participles, is in the objective case."

Care is a *noun*; *common*; *neuter gender*; *third person*; *singular number*; *objective case*; it is used as the object of the preposition "with." Rule VII. "The object of a preposition is in the objective case."

Analyze the following sentences, and parse the nouns.

1. Borneo is a large island. 2. Our father lives in Washington. 3. John's dog bit Clarence. 4. Johnson's farm is mortgaged. 5. Mr. Trowel the mason is ill. 6. The statue fell from its pedestal. 7. Gad, a troop shall overcome him. 8. Jocko has stolen my glasses. 9. Susan's mother is my aunt. 10. Is the doctor's office open?

11. Next to sincerity, remember still
Thou must resolve upon *integrity*.
God will have all thou hast; thy mind, thy will,
Thy thoughts, thy words, thy works.—*Herbert*.

Correct the following sentences. Consult your dictionary as needed.

1. Jane has two brother-in-laws. 2. Three chimnies were on fire. 3. The Shaker's are industrious. 4. Did you attend Mr. Chance' lecture. 5. I called at Coleman's the jeweler's. 6. She is reading in her sister's Mary's book. 7. The boys coat is torn. 8. How many of the Johnson's were there? 9. The mens' wages should be paid today. 10. He has quartoes and folioes in his library.

59. COMPOSITION

Write a description of a squirrel, using the following plan.

Plan—1. Size, as compared with some other small animal. 2. Form, noting particularly its teeth, claws, and tail. 3. Habits, nest, and food. 4. Its disposition, whether timid or bold, etc. 5. Different kinds, and their peculiarities. 6. Migrations. 7. Enemies.

Write descriptions of some of the following animals, using this general plan.

General Plan—1. Size. 2. Form, noting marked features. 3. Color. 4. Food. 5. Habits. 6. Disposition. 7. Where found. 8. Remarks, anecdotes, etc.

Rem.—The pupil should be permitted and encouraged to vary the order in which the topics are arranged in this plan and to introduce such other topics as seem necessary to complete the description of any animal.

The dog	The shark	The turkey	The elephant
The owl	The horse	The pigeon	The muskrat
The bee	The crow	The mouse	The mosquito

Parse the nouns in your compositions.

60. PROPERTIES OF THE PRONOUN

To pronouns belong *gender*, *number*, *person*, and *case*.

61. PERSONAL PRONOUNS

1. The **simple personal pronouns** are *I*, *you*, *he*, *she*, and *it*, with their declined forms *we*, *our*, *us*, *my*, *mine*, *you*, *your*, *his*, *him*, *her*, *its*, *they*, *their*, *them*.

2. The **compound personal pronouns** are formed by adding *self* or *selves* to some form of the simple personals; as, *myself*, *yourselves*, *himself*, *themselves*.

Rem. 1—*You* is used to represent both singular and plural nouns.

Rem. 2—*We* is used in place of *I*, in editorials, royal proclamations, etc.; as "*We*, James, King of Great Britain," "*We* were mistaken."

Rem. 3—*It* is sometimes used in the nominative, without reference to any particular antecedent, and in the objective for euphony alone or to supply the place of some indefinite object; as "*It* is raining," "Come and trip *it* on the green."

Rem. 4—When pronouns of different persons are used, the *second* should precede the *third*, and the *third* should precede the *first*.

62. DECLENSION OF PERSONAL PRONOUNS

FIRST PERSON

	Singular	Plural		Singular	Plural
Nom.	I	We	Nom.	Myself	Ourselves
Poss.	My, mine	Our	Poss.	_____	_____
Obj.	Me	Us	Obj.	Myself	Ourselves

SECOND PERSON

	Singular	Plural		Singular	Plural
Nom.	You	You	Nom.		
Poss.	Your	Your	and	Yourself	Yourselves
Obj.	You	You	Obj.		

THIRD PERSON

	Singular				Plural
	MASC.	FEM.	NEUT.		COM. OR NEUT.
Nom.	He	She	It	Nom.	They
Poss.	His	Her	Its	Poss.	Their
Obj.	Him	Her	It	Obj.	Them

	Singular		Plural
	MASC.		
Nom.	Himself	Nom.	
and	FEM.	and	COM. OR NEUT.
Obj.	Herself	Obj.	Themselves
	NEUT.		
	Itself		

63. ORDER OF PARSING

1. A pronoun, and why? 2. Personal, and why? 3. What is its antecedent? 4. Gender, person, and number? Rule. 5. Decline it. 6. Case, and why? Rule.

64. MODELS FOR PARSING

I. "I see them coming up the street."

I is a *pronoun*; *personal*; it shows by its form that it is of the first person: its antecedent is the name, understood, of the speaker—*gender, first person, singular number*, to agree with its antecedent. Rule IX. "Pronouns must agree with their antecedents in gender, person, and number." Decline it: *nominative case*: Rule I.

Them is a *pronoun*; *personal*; its antecedent is the name, understood, of the person spoken of—*gender, third person, plural number*: Rule IX. Decline it: *objective case*, it is the object of the transitive verb "see": Rule VI.

II. "I myself told you so."

Myself is a *pronoun*; *personal*; *compound*: its antecedent is the name, understood, of the speaker—*gender, first person, singular number*: Rule IX. Decline it: *nominative case*, in apposition with "I": Rule IV.

*Analyze the following sentences, and parse the **nouns** and **personal pronouns**.*

1. You and he are my friends. 2. I saw them in their convertible. 3. The soldiers helped themselves. 4. You are the man. 5. He saved your money for you. 6. Your father knows us. 7. He himself hid your baseball.

8. Where shall I see him? angels tell me where.
You know him; he is near you; point him out.
Shall I see glories beaming from his brow,
Or trace his footsteps by the rising flowers?—*Young.*

*Write the first two sentences of a composition on "The Bald Eagle," and parse the **personal pronouns**.*

Finish the composition.

Questions—What is a pronoun? A personal pronoun? What are the simple personal pronouns? The compound personal pronouns? What does "you" represent? How is "we" used? How is "it" sometimes used? Give examples of the use of these pronouns. When pronouns of different persons are used, how should they be arranged? Decline the personal pronouns. Repeat the order of parsing personal pronouns.

65. POSSESSIVE PRONOUNS

1. The **possessive pronouns** are *mine, his, hers, ours, yours, theirs.*

2. To denote emphatic distinction, *my own* is used for *mine, his own* for *his, our own* for *ours, your own* for *yours, their own* for *theirs.*

66. ORDER OF PARSING

1. A pronoun, and why? 2. Possessive, and why? 3. What is its antecedent? 4. Gender, person, number, and why? Rule. 5. Case, and why? Rule.

67. MODELS FOR PARSING

I. "That book is mine, not yours."

FIRST METHOD

Mine is a *pronoun, possessive*; it represents both the possessor and the thing possessed: it's antecedent is "book": *neuter gender, third person, singular number*, to agree with its antecedent (Rule IX); *nominative case*; it is used as the predicate of the proposition (Rule II). Parse "yours" in a similar manner.

SECOND METHOD

Mine is a *pronoun, possessive*; it is equivalent to "my book." Parse "my" as a personal pronoun in the possessive case, according to Rule III, and "book" as a predicate nominative, according to Rule II.

Analyze the following sentences and parse the possessive pronouns.

1. That horse of yours is lame. 2. This sled is not yours: it must be hers. 3. The money is your own. 4. Friend of mine, you are welcome. 5. That garden of theirs is a very fine one. 6. This book is not mine; it must be his or hers. 7. She is an old friend of ours. 8. These books are yours, not theirs. 9. We love this land of ours. 10. The boy left his hat and took mine. 11. You should study your own books and not borrow hers.

Questions—What is a possessive pronoun? Name the possessive pronouns. How is emphatic distinction denoted? Repeat the order of parsing possessive pronouns.

68. RELATIVE PRONOUNS

1. The **simple relative pronouns** are *who, which, what*, and *that*.

Rem.—*That* is a relative when *who, which*, or *whom* can be used in its place. *As* is used as a relative pronoun after *such, many*, and *same*.

2. The **compound relative pronouns** are *whoever, whoso, whosoever, whichever, whichsoever, whatever*, and *whatsoever*.

Rem.—*Whosoever, whichsoever*, and *whatsoever* are emphatic forms of *whoever, whichever*, and *whatever*.

Ex.—"I'll have nothing *whatsoever* to do with the matter." "*Whosoever* will may come to the Lord."

3. Some relative pronouns not only connect clauses, but also comprise in themselves both antecedent and relative. These are called **double relatives**, and they may be either simple or compound.

In the sentence, "I got what I desired," *what* is a double relative, and is used instead of *the thing which*—"I got *the thing which* I desired." "Thing," the object of "got," is the antecedent, and is modified by "the" and "which I desired," both adjective elements.

In the sentence, "Tell what you know," *what* is a double relative, and is equivalent to *that which*—"Tell *that which* you know." "That," the object of "tell," is the antecedent, and is modified by "which you know," an adjective element.

In the sentence, "Whatever is, is right," *whatever* is a double relative, and is equivalent to *that which*—"*That which* is, is right." "That," the subject of the proposition, "That is right," is the antecedent, and "that," the subject, is modified by "which is," an adjective element.

In the sentence, "Whoever runs may read," *whoever* is equivalent to *he who*, or *any person who*—"*He who* runs may read." "He," the subject of the sentence, "He may read," is the antecedent of "who," and is modified by "who runs," an adjective element.

In the sentence, "Whichever road you may take will lead to the city," *whichever* is equivalent to *any which*—"*Any* road *which* you may take," etc. "Any" and "which you may take" are adjective elements, modifying "road," the antecedent of "which."

69. DECLENSION

	Singular and Plural		Singular and Plural
Nom.	Who	*Nom.*	Which
Poss.	Whose	*Poss.*	Whose
Obj.	Whom	*Obj.*	Which

70. ORDER OF PARSING

1. A pronoun, and why? 2. Relative, and why? 3. Name its antecedent. 4. Gender, person, and number? Rule. 5. Decline it. 6. Case and rule.

71. MODELS FOR PARSING

I. "Happy is the man that findeth wisdom."

That is a *pronoun*; *relative*; it represents a preceding word or phrase, to which it joins a limiting clause: its antecedent is "man": *masculine gender*, *third person*, *singular number*: Rule IX: *nominative case*; it is the subject of the relative clause, "That findeth wisdom": Rule I.

II. "Whoever perseveres will succeed."

Whoever is a *pronoun*; *relative*; it is equivalent to *he who*, or *anyone who*—"he" being the antecedent, and "who" the relative. Parse "he" as a personal pronoun, subject of "will succeed," or "one" as an adjective used as a noun, subject of "will succeed," and "who" as a relative, subject of "perseveres," according to Rule I.

III. "I remember what you said."

What is a *pronoun*; *relative*; it is equivalent to *that which*—"that" being the antecedent part, and "which" the relative. Parse "that" as an adjective used as a noun, in the objective case after "remember."

Which is a *pronoun*; *relative*; its antecedent is "that": *neuter gender, third person, singular number*: Rule IX: *objective case*; object of the transitive verb "said": Rule VI.

Analyze the following sentences, and parse the pronouns.

1. He who hates deceives with his lips. 2. This is the child who was lost. 3. The dog which you bought was stolen. 4. He will do what is right. 5. Ask for what you want. 6. That is the man whose house was burned. 7. This is the dog that worried the cat that killed the rat that ate the malt that lay in the house that Jack built.

Write the first two sentences of a composition on "The Quail," and parse the nouns and pronouns.

Now, finish the composition.

Questions—What is a relative pronoun? What are the simple relatives? The compound relatives? What are double relatives? To what is "what" equivalent? "Whatever?" "Whoever?" "Whichever?" "Whoso" and "Whosoever?" *Ans.*—He who. Decline "who" and "which." Repeat the order of parsing a relative pronoun.

72. INTERROGATIVE PRONOUNS

1. The **interrogative pronouns** are *who*, *which*, and *what*, when used in asking questions.

2. The **subsequent** of an interrogative pronoun is that part of the answer which it represents.

Rem.—An interrogative pronoun must agree with its subsequent in gender, person and number. When the answer is not given or clearly implied, its gender and person are indeterminate, and it is in the singular number.

Ex.—"Who is hurt?" The answer to this question not being given, it is evident that the gender and person of "who" are indeterminate.

"Who is hurt? Mike." The answer to this question is given. "Who" is masculine gender, third person, singular number, agreeing with "Mike," its subsequent.

Apply Rule IX in parsing interrogatives, changing "antecedent" to "subsequent."

73. ORDER OF PARSING

1. A pronoun, and why? 2. Interrogative, and why? 3. Name its subsequent, if expressed. 4. Gender, person, and number? Rule. 5. Decline it. 6. Case and rule.

74. MODELS FOR PARSING

I. "Who invented gunpowder?"

Who is a *pronoun*, *interrogative*; it is used in asking a question: its subsequent is not expressed: *gender*, *person*, and *number* indeterminate: *nominative case*; it is used as the subject of the proposition: Rule I.

II. "What is that man? A lawyer."

What is a *pronoun*, *interrogative*; its subsequent is "lawyer"; *masculine gender*, *third person*, *singular number*: Rule IX: *nominative case*; it is used as the predicate of the proposition: Rule II.

Analyze the following sentences and parse the pronouns.

1. Who came with you? 2. Whose horse ran away? 3. Whom did you call? Mary. 4. What did you say? 5. What is that? It is a bicycle. 6. Which will you have? The large one. 7. Who told you how to parse "what"?

Questions—What are the interrogative pronouns? What is the subsequent of an interrogative? With what must an interrogative agree in gender, person, and number? Repeat the order of parsing an interrogative.

75. FALSE SYNTAX

False syntax is any violation of the laws of good usage in the application of words or the construction of sentences.

76. CAUTIONS

Caution I—Do not **omit the subjects** of clauses or declarative sentences as in these incorrect examples.

Ex.—1. Glad you have come. 2. Hope you will remain long with us. 3. What say? 4. It was Johnson saved the drowning man. 5. After a long hike felt very much fatigued. 6. Read his poems; like them very much.

Caution II—Do not use **who** as the object of a transitive verb or preposition.

Ex.—1. Do you know whom you are talking to? 2. He is a fellow whom I do not like. 3. Tell me whom you work for.

Rem.—If the statement makes sense with an object-form pronoun at the end or following the preposition, use *whom*. If it does not make sense that way, use *who*. For example, I do not like *him* (objective—use *whom*); Tell me for *whom* (objective) you work.

Caution III—The second person should **precede** the third, and the third should precede the first.

Ex—1. You and he are in the same class. 2. You and I will not whisper. 3. He and I went skating.

Caution IV—Do not use a pronoun and its antecedent as **subjects of the same proposition** as in these incorrect examples.

Ex.—1. Mr. Kellogg he has bought our farm. 2. Many words they darken speech. 3. The boys they all stayed in at recess. 4. The horse he ran and the man he yelled "whoa."

Review "Cautions" in Section 35.

Correct the following sentences by reference to Rule IX.

1. Every person should mind their own business. 2. Each day has their own anxieties. 3. If anyone hasn't voted, they should raise their hands. 4. Many a youth have injured their health by keeping late hours.

Questions—What is false syntax? Repeat the cautions.

77. DESCRIPTIVE ADJECTIVES

Most descriptive adjectives, by change of form or the addition of modifying words, express quality in different degrees. This is called *comparison*.

1. **Comparison** is a variation of the adjective to express different degrees of quality; as, *rich, richer, richest*.

2. There are three **degrees of comparison:** *positive, comparative*, and *superlative*.

3. The **positive degree** expresses the simple quality, or an equal degree of the quality; as, "An old man," "She is as *good* as she is *beautiful*."

Rem.—The suffix *ish*, and the words *rather*, *somewhat*, etc., express a small amount of the quality; as, *greenish*, slightly green; *rather* warm, *somewhat* awkward.

4. The **comparative degree** ascribes to one of two objects a higher or lower degree of the quality than that expressed by the positive; as, "An *older* man;" "Charles is *more studious* than Mary."

Rem.—The comparative of monosyllables is regularly formed by adding *r* or *er* to the positive: the comparative of adjectives of more than one syllable is formed by prefixing *more* or *less* to the positive; as, *rough*, *rougher*; *more honorable*, *less honorable*.

5. The **superlative degree** ascribes the highest or lowest degree of the quality to one of more than two objects; as, "The *oldest* man;" "The *least fertile* farm in the township."

Rem. 1—The superlative of monosyllables is regularly formed by adding *st* or *est* to the positive: of adjectives of more than one syllable, by prefixing *most* or *least* to the positive; as, *roughest*, *most honorable*, *least honorable*.

Rem. 2—Some adjectives are compared irregularly; as, *good*, *better*, *best*; *bad*, *worse*, *worst*.

Rem. 3—Some adjectives cannot be compared since they represent an absolute degree; as, *square*, *infinite*, *supreme*.

Rem. 4—Adjectives should not be doubly compared.

Compare the following adjectives.

far	holy	great	honest	cheerful
old	loud	proud	narrow	studious
near	much	angry	skillful	agreeable
wise	little	young	sensible	laughable

*Tell the **degree of comparison** of the following adjectives.*

most	taller	infirm	most useful	most hurtful
later	eldest	stormy	rather nice	very frightful
better	richer	farthest	less studious	less confident
round	perfect	greenest	more hopeful	least sensible

Questions—What is a comparison? How many degrees of comparison are there? What does the positive degree express? The comparative? The superlative? How are the comparative and superlative degrees formed?

78. DEFINITIVE ADJECTIVES

1. **Pronominal adjectives** are those definitives, most of which may, without the article prefixed, represent a noun understood.

The principal pronominals are:
1. The **demonstratives**, *this, that, these, those, former, latter, both, same, yonder.*
2. The **distributives**, *each, every, either, neither.*
3. The **indefinites**, *all, any, another, certain, enough, few, little, many, much, no, none, one, own, other, several, some, which, whichever, whichsoever, what, whatever, whatsoever.*

Rem. 1—The phrases *such a, many a, what a, but a, only a,* etc., may be called pronominals, and be parsed as single words.

Rem. 2—Some pronominals can be compared like descriptive adjectives; as, *few, fewer, fewest; much, more, most.*

2. **Numeral adjectives** are those definitives which denote number and order definitely; as, *two, fourth, fourfold.*

There are three classes of numeral adjectives: *cardinal, ordinal,* and *multiplicative.*
1. **Cardinals** denote the number of objects; as, *two, four, a thousand.*
2. **Ordinals** mark the position of an object in a series; as, *second, fourth, thousandth.*
3. **Multiplicatives** denote how many fold; as, *twofold, fourfold.*

79. ORDER OF PARSING

1. An adjective, and why? 2. Descriptive or definitive, and why? 3. Compare it, if it admits of comparison. 4. Degree of comparison? 5. What does it modify? Rule.

80. MODELS FOR PARSING

I. "Fearful storms sweep over these islands."

Fearful is an *adjective, descriptive*; it modifies a noun by denoting some quality: *compared, pos.* fearful, *com.* more fearful, *sup.* most fearful: *positive degree*, and belongs to "storms." Rule XII. "An adjective or participle belongs to some noun or pronoun."

These is an *adjective, definitive*; it defines without denoting any quality: it cannot be compared, and belongs to "islands:" Rule XII.

II. "I have been there many a time."

Many a is an *adjective, definitive*; it cannot be compared, and belongs to "time;" Rule XII.

*Analyze the following sentences, and parse the **nouns, pronouns, and adjectives**.*

1. I saw a large herd of cattle. 2. Jane is studying modern history. 3. Fido is a Newfoundland dog. 4. You may have the largest lemon. 5. Every man received a penny. 6. Either road leads to town. 7. That course was most honorable. 8. He took a twofold view of the subject. 9. What is that noise? 10. Two men wanted the fourth horse.

11. Alas for those who never sing,
But die with all their music in them.—*Holmes.*

12. With many a curve my banks I fret,
By many a field and fallow,
And many a fairy foreland, set
With willow, weed, and mallow.—*Tennyson.*

Questions—Define pronominal adjectives. Name the principal demonstratives. Distributives. Indefinites. What phrases may be regarded as pronominals? What pronominals can be compared? What are numeral adjectives? Name and define the three classes of numeral adjectives. Repeat the order of parsing an adjective.

81. CAUTIONS

Caution I—Avoid **double comparatives** and **superlatives.**

Ex.—1. He is the most miserablest man in town. 2. No man can't be more neutraler than I on political issues. 3. He seems more cheerfuller today. 4. That is more preferable than to be imprisoned.

Caution II—Omit the article **before a word used as a title,** or as a **mere name.**

Ex.—1. They gave him the title of (an) emperor. 2. They elected him as (a) chairman.

Caution III—Place **ordinal adjectives** before **cardinals** in most constructions.

Ex.—Incorrect: Sing the two first and two last verses. Correct: Sing the first two and the last two verses.

Caution IV—Plural adjectives should modify **plural** nouns; **singular** adjectives, **singular** nouns.

Ex.—Incorrect: I do not like these kind of apples. Correct: I do not like this kind (or these kinds) of apples.

82. COMPOSITION

Write a composition on "The Peach Tree," using the following plan.

Plan—1. Size, as compared with the apple tree. 2. Form, division of branches. 3. Color of leaves in spring and fall. 4. Appearance when in bloom. 5. Is it found wild? If so, where? 6. What part of the fruit is eaten? 7. Different kinds of peaches.

Write compositions on some of the plants named below using the following general plan.

General Plan—1. Size, as compared with some other plant. 2. Form, noting important parts. 3. Wild or cultivated—where found wild. 4. If useful, how protected or cultivated. 5. What parts are used for food or for manufacturing purposes.

The pine	The violet	The hickory	The rosebush
The tulip	The beech	The chestnut	The wheat plant
The daisy	The maple	The dogwood	The tomato plant

Questions—What is an adjective? A descriptive adjective? What is comparison? What is a definitive adjective? What are pronominal adjectives? What are numeral adjectives? Cardinals? Ordinals? Multiplicatives?

Review the cautions of Section 81.

83. PROPERTIES OF THE VERB

To verbs belong *voice*, *mode*, *tense*, *number*, and *person*.

Let the pupil now review Sections 15, 16, and 25.

84. VOICE

A verb may represent its subject as acting or as being acted upon. In the sentence, "John struck James," "John," the subject, is represented as acting: in the sentence, "James was struck by John," "James," the subject, is represented as being acted upon. This property is called *voice*, and is peculiar to *transitive* verbs.

1. **Voice** is that form of the transitive verb which shows whether the subject acts or is acted upon.

2. Transitive verbs have two voices: an *active* and a *passive voice.*

3. The **active voice** represents the subject as acting upon an object; as, "The boy *wrote* a letter."

4. The **passive voice** represents the subject as being acted upon; as, "The letter *was written.*"

5. The passive voice is formed by prefixing some form of the verb *to be* to the perfect participle of a transitive verb.

Rem. 1—When a verb in the active voice is changed into the passive, the direct object in the active becomes the subject in the passive; as, "The cat *caught* the mouse" (*active*); "The mouse *was caught* by the cat" (*passive*).

Rem. 2—Active voice sentences are more forceful than passive voice, and ordinarily more interesting, so use it as much as possible.

*Tell which verbs are **active** and which **passive** in the following exercises.*

1. The girl sings. 2. Fire burns. 3. The mail was robbed. 4. A meteor was seen. 5. He should have told the truth. 6. Children love play. 7. He has found his knife. 8. A watch was found in the street. 9. The burglar might have been arrested.

Questions—What is a verb? A transitive verb? An intransitive verb? A copulative verb?

What is a participle? The present participle? How does the present participle always end? What is the perfect participle? How does it usually end? What is the compound participle? How is it formed?

What belong to verbs? What is voice? How many voices have transitive verbs? What is the active voice? The passive voice? How is the passive voice formed? How is a verb in the active voice changed into the passive? Give examples.

85. MODE

1. **Mode** is the manner in which the action, being, or state is expressed.

2. There are five modes: *indicative, subjunctive, potential, imperative,* and *infinitive.*

3. The **indicative mode** asserts a thing as a *fact,* or as *actually existing*; as, "Fire *burns,*" "A battle *was fought.*"

4. The **subjunctive mode** asserts a thing as *doubtful,* as a *supposition,* or denies the fact supposed; as, "If this *be* true, all will end well," "I shall go, if you *remain.*"

5. The **potential mode** asserts the *power, necessity, liberty, duty,* or *liability* of acting, or of being in a certain state; as, "He *can talk,*" "You *must go,*" "They *should be* more careful."

Rem.—*May, can, must, might, could, would,* and *should* are the *signs* of the potential mode.

6. The **imperative mode** expresses a *command,* an *exhortation,* an *entreaty,* or a *permission*; as, "*Go,*" "*Do* not *hurt* me."

7. The **infinitive mode** expresses the action, being, or state, without affirming it; as, "*To go*" "He wants *to speak.*"

Rem. 1—The infinitive may usually be known by the sign *to* placed before it. This sign is omitted after the words *bid, dare, feel, help, let, make, need, see,* and a few others; as, "*Let* them [to] *come* on," "*See* him [to] *run,*" "*Bid* them [to] *come.*"

Rem. 2—The indicative and potential modes may be used in asking questions; as, "*Is* he honest?" "*Has* she *arrived*?" "*May* I *go* home?"

Tell the mode of the verbs in the following sentences.

1. The army encamped by the river. 2. Run for some water. 3. You must recite your lesson. 4. I will recite my lesson if I can. 5. I like to play. 6. Hope thou in God. 7. Do let me go to the picnic. 8. He should have come home. 9. Lift up your heads, O ye gates! 10. Were I rich, I would purchase that property.

Write a description of "The Oak," and tell the modes of the verbs used.

Questions—What is mode? How many modes are there? Name them. What is the indicative mode? What is the subjunctive mode? What is the potential mode? What are the signs of the potential mode? What is the imperative mode? The infinitive mode? What is the sign of the infinitive mode? What modes are used in asking questions?

86. TENSE

1. **Tense** denotes the time of an action or event.

2. There are six tenses: the *present,* the *present perfect,* the *past,* the *past perfect,* the *future,* and the *future perfect.*

3. The **present tense** denotes present time; as, "I *write,*" "The wind *is blowing.*"

4. The **present perfect tense** represents an action or event as past but connected with present time; as, "I *have written,*" "The wind *has been blowing.*"

5. The **past tense** denotes past time; as, "I *wrote*," "The wind *blew*."

6. The **past perfect tense** represents an act as ended or completed in time fully past; as, "I *had written*," "The bridge *had fallen* before we reached it."

7. The **future tense** denotes future time; as, "I *shall write*," "The lion *shall eat* straw like the ox."

8. The **future perfect tense** represents an act as finished or ended at or before a certain future time; as, "I *shall have written* the letter before the mail goes out."

87. SIGNS OF THE TENSES: ACTIVE VOICE

INDICATIVE MODE

Present . . . . Simple form of the verb.
Past . . . . When regular, add *ed* to the simple form.
Future . . . . Prefix *shall* or *will* to the simple form.
Present Perfect . . . . . Prefix *have* or *has* to the perfect participle.
Past Perfect . . . . Prefix *had* to the perfect participle.
Future Perfect . . . . . Prefix *shall have* or *will have* to the perfect participle.

SUBJUNCTIVE MODE

If, though, except, unless, etc., placed before tense forms given in the conjugation.

POTENTIAL MODE

Present . . . . Prefix *may, can,* or *must* to the simple form.
Past . . . . Prefix *might, could, would,* or *should* to the simple form.
Present Perfect . . . . . Prefix *may have, can have,* or *must have* to the perfect participle.
Past Perfect . . . . Prefix *might have, could have, would have,* or *should have* to the perfect participle.

IMPERATIVE MODE

Present . . . . *Let,* or a command.

INFINITIVE MODE

Present .... Prefix *to* to the simple form.
Present Perfect ... Prefix *to have* to the perfect participle.

PARTICIPLES

Present .... Add *ing* to the simple form.
Perfect .... When regular, add *ed* or *d* to the simple form.
Compound .... Prefix *having* to the perfect participle, or *having been* to the present active or perfect participle.

*Tell the **tense** of the verbs in the following sentences.*

1. Debbie sings. 2. I went home. 3. John ran. 4. Write. 5. Let him go. 6. The man shouted. 7. I had been taught. 8. They will succeed. 9. We shall be glad. 10. The letter will have been written. 11. If you go, I shall stay. 12. You might study. 13. He may have written.

Write a description of "The Pine," and tell the modes and tenses of the verbs used.

Questions—What is tense? How many tenses are there? What is the present tense? The present perfect? The past? The past perfect? The future? The future perfect? Give the signs of the tenses.

88. PERSON AND NUMBER

1. The **person** and **number** of verbs are the changes which they undergo to mark their agreement with their subjects.

2. A verb must agree with its subject in person and number.

Rem.—The infinitive, having no subject, has neither person nor number.

89. AUXILIARIES

Auxiliary verbs are those which are used in the conjugation of other verbs. They are *do, be, have, shall, will, may, can, must.*

Rem.—*Do, be, have,* and *will* are often used as principal verbs; as, "He *does* well," "I *am*," "He *has* money," "He *wills* it."

Questions—What is meant by the person and number of a verb? With what must a verb agree in person and number? What are auxiliary verbs? Which of them are sometimes used as principal verbs?

90. CONJUGATION

1. The **conjugation** of a verb is the correct expression, in regular order, of its *modes*, *tenses*, *voices*, *persons*, and *numbers*.

2. The **principal parts** of a verb are the *present indicative*, the *past indicative*, and the *perfect participle*.

91. CONJUGATION OF THE VERB "TO BE"
PRINCIPAL PARTS

Present Tense	*Past Tense*	*Perfect Participle*
Be, or am	Was	Been

INDICATIVE MODE

PRESENT TENSE

Singular
1. I am
2. You are
3. He is

Plural
1. We are
2. You are
3. They are

PRESENT PERFECT TENSE

1. I have been
2. You have been
3. He has been

1. We have been
2. You have been
3. They have been

PAST TENSE

1. I was
2. You were
3. He was

1. We were
2. You were
3. They were

PAST PERFECT TENSE

1. I had been
2. You had been
3. He had been

1. We had been
2. You had been
3. They had been

FUTURE TENSE

1. I shall be
2. You will be
3. He will be

1. We shall be
2. You will be
3. They will be

FUTURE PERFECT TENSE

Singular
1. I shall have been
2. You will have been
3. He will have been

Plural
1. We shall have been
2. You will have been
3. They will have been

SUBJUNCTIVE MODE

PRESENT TENSE

1. If I be
2. If you be
3. If he be

1. If we be
2. If you be
3. If they be

PAST TENSE

1. If I were
2. If you were
3. If he were

1. If we were
2. If you were
3. If they were

PAST PERFECT TENSE

1. If I had been
2. If you had been
3. If he had been

1. If we had been
2. If you had been
3. If they had been

POTENTIAL MODE

PRESENT TENSE

1. I may be
2. You may be
3. He may be

1. We may be
2. You may be
3. They may be

PRESENT PERFECT TENSE

1. I may have been
2. You may have been
3. He may have been

1. We may have been
2. You may have been
3. They may have been

PAST TENSE

1. I might be
2. You might be
3. He might be

1. We might be
2. You might be
3. They might be

PAST PERFECT TENSE

Singular	*Plural*
1. I might have been	1. We might have been
2. You might have been	2. You might have been
3. He might have been	3. They might have been

Note—In reviews, use the auxiliary *can* or *must*.

IMPERATIVE MODE

PRESENT TENSE

1. Be   2. Be

INFINITIVE MODE

Present, To be   *Present Perfect*, To have been

PARTICIPLES

Present, Being   *Perfect*, Been   *Compound*, Having been

Note—*Shall*, in the first person, and *will*, in the second and third, future tenses, are used to denote *futurity*. When *will* is used in the first person, or *shall*, in the second or third, *determination* or *necessity*, as well as *futurity*, is represented.

A **synopsis** of a verb shows its variations in form, through the different voices, modes, and tenses, in a single person and number.

Write a synopsis of the verb "to be" in the first person, singular number.

92. CONJUGATION OF THE VERB "TO LOVE"
ACTIVE VOICE
PRINCIPAL PARTS

Present Tense	*Past Tense*	*Perfect Participle*
Love	Loved	Loved

INDICATIVE MODE

PRESENT TENSE

Singular	*Plural*
1. I love	1. We love
2. You love	2. You love
3. He loves	3. They love

PRESENT PERFECT TENSE

Singular	*Plural*
1. I have loved	1. We have loved
2. You have loved	2. You have loved
3. He has loved	3. They have loved

PAST TENSE

1. I loved	1. We loved
2. You loved	2. You loved
3. He loved	3. They loved

PAST PERFECT TENSE

1. I had loved	1. We had loved
2. You had loved	2. You had loved
3. He had loved	3. They had loved

FUTURE TENSE

1. I shall love	1. We shall love
2. You will love	2. You will love
3. He will love	3. They will love

FUTURE PERFECT TENSE

1. I shall have loved	1. We shall have loved
2. You will have loved	2. You will have loved
3. He will have loved	3. They will have loved

SUBJUNCTIVE MODE

PRESENT TENSE

1. If I love	1. If we love
2. If you love	2. If you love
3. If he love	3. If they love

PAST TENSE

1. If I loved	1. If we loved
2. If you loved	2. If you loved
3. If he loved	3. If they loved

PAST PERFECT TENSE

1. If I had loved	1. If we had loved
2. If you had loved	2. If you had loved
3. If he had loved	3. If they had loved

POTENTIAL MODE

PRESENT TENSE

Singular	*Plural*
1. I may love	1. We may love
2. You may love	2. You may love
3. He may love	3. They may love

PRESENT PERFECT TENSE

1. I may have loved	1. We may have loved
2. You may have loved	2. You may have loved
3. He may have loved	3. They may have loved

PAST TENSE

1. I might love	1. We might love
2. You might love	2. You might love
3. He might love	3. They might love

PAST PERFECT TENSE

1. I might have loved	1. We might have loved
2. You might have loved	2. You might have loved
3. He might have loved	3. They might have loved

IMPERATIVE MODE

2. Love   2. Love

INFINITIVE MODE

Present, To love   *Present Perfect*, To have loved

PARTICIPLES

Present, Loving   *Perfect*, Loved   *Compound*, Having loved

93. SYNOPSIS OF THE VERB "TO LOVE"

PASSIVE VOICE

The **passive voice** is formed by prefixing the various forms of the verb *to be*, to the *perfect participle*.

INDICATIVE MODE

Present .... I am loved
Present Perfect ..... I have been loved
Past .... I was loved
Past Perfect .... I had been loved
Future .... I shall be loved
Future Perfect ..... I shall have been loved

SUBJUNCTIVE MODE

Present ....If I be loved   *Past* ....If I were loved
Past Perfect . . . If I had been loved

POTENTIAL MODE

Present .... I may be loved
Present Perfect ..... I may have been loved
Past .... I might be loved
Past Perfect .... I might have been loved

IMPERATIVE MODE

Present .... Be loved

INFINITIVE MODE

Present, To be loved   *Present Perfect*, To have been loved

PARTICIPLES

Present, Being loved   *Perfect*, Loved   *Compound*, Having been loved

94. COORDINATE FORMS OF CONJUGATION

1. The progressive, the emphatic, and the interrogative are called the *coordinate forms of conjugation*.

2. The **progressive form** is used to denote action, being, or state in progress; as, "He *was writing*."

In the progressive form, the various forms of the verb *to be* are prefixed to the *present active participle*.

3. The **emphatic form** represents an act with emphasis; as, "I *do write,*" "He *did write.*"

4. The **interrogative form** is used in asking questions; as, "*Love* I?" "*Did* he *write?*"

PROGRESSIVE FORM—SYNOPSIS

INDICATIVE MODE

Present . . . . I am loving
Present Perfect . . . . . I have been loving
Past . . . . I was loving
Past Perfect . . . . I had been loving
Future . . . . I shall be loving
Future Perfect . . . . . I shall have been loving

SUBJUNCTIVE MODE

Present . . . If I be loving   *Past* . . . If I were loving
Past Perfect . . . . If I had been loving

POTENTIAL MODE

Present . . . . I may be loving
Present Perfect . . . . . I may have been loving
Past . . . . I might be loving
Past Perfect . . . . I might have been loving

INFINITIVE MODE

Present, To be loving   *Present Perfect*, To have been loving

IMPERATIVE MODE

Present . . . Be loving

PARTICIPLES

Present, Loving   *Compound*, Having been loving

THE EMPHATIC FORM—SYNOPSIS

INDICATIVE MODE

Present . . . I do love   *Past* . . . I did love

SUBJUNCTIVE MODE

Present . . . If I do love   *Past* . . . If I did love

IMPERATIVE MODE

Present . . . . Do thou love

INTERROGATIVE FORM—SYNOPSIS

INDICATIVE MODE

Present . . . . Love I? Do I love? Am I loving?
Present Perfect . . . . Have I loved? Have I been loving?
Past . . . . Loved I? Did I love? Was I loving?
Past Perfect . . . . Had I loved? Had I been loving?
Future . . . . Shall I love? Shall I be loving?
Future Perfect . . . . . Shall I have loved? Shall I have been loving?

POTENTIAL MODE

Present . . . . Must I love?
Present Perfect . . . . . Must I have loved?
Past . . . . Might I love?
Past Perfect . . . . Might I have loved?

Write a synopsis of the transitive verbs *think*, *instruct*, *command*, *punish*, *teach*, and *see*, in the indicative, subjunctive, and potential modes, active and passive voices.

*Tell the **mode, tense, person,** and **number** of each verb in the following sentences.*

1. He ran. 2. You teach. 3. They have seen. 4. If he go. 5. They may have written. 6. Has he departed. 7. They will command. 8. Nancy will have recited. 9. The army will be disbanded.

10. America was discovered. 11. The people should be contented. 12. He has built a trail bike. 13. Attend to your lesson. 14. He can go if the bus is not too full. 15. The man loves to see it rain.

Write a description called "The Riding Horse" and parse the verbs.

Questions—What is conjugation? What are the principal parts of a verb? What is the synopsis of a verb? Give the synopsis of "to be." Of "to love" in both the active and the passive voice. How is the passive voice formed? What are the coordinate forms of conjugation? What is the progressive form? The emphatic form? The interrogative form? Give the synopsis of each form.

95. REGULAR AND IRREGULAR VERBS

1. A **regular verb** forms its past indicative and perfect participle by adding *d* or *ed* to the present indicative; as, *love, love-d, love-d; count, count-ed, count-ed.*

2. An **irregular verb** is one which does not form its past tense and perfect participle by adding *d* or *ed* to the present indicative; as, *go, went, gone; see, saw, seen; do, did, done.*

For list of irregular verbs see Appendix.

96. DEFECTIVE AND REDUNDANT VERBS

1. **Defective verbs** are those which are missing some of the principal parts. They include *aware, ought,* and *beware* from *be.*

2. **Redundant verbs** are those which have more than one form for their past tense or perfect participle; as, *cleave, clove,* or *clave; cleft, cloven,* or *cleaved.*

Correct the following sentences, using this model.

MODEL

"The man throwed a stone."

This sentence is incorrect. The word "throwed" should be "threw," the past indicative of the verb "throw." The sentence should read, "The man threw a stone."

1. I have saw some fine cattle today. 2. He ought to have went home. 3. The beads were stringed on a silk thread.

4. He has brung some snow into the schoolhouse. 5. The cloth was weaved by hand. 6. The horse come cantering along. 7. This coat has wore well.

8. The cars have ran off the track. 9. The bells ringed when the news was got. 10. I clumb the tree and shaked the apples off. 11. The candle should be blowed out. 12. I laid down. 13. Was the cow drove to pasture? 14. The plastering has fell from the ceiling.

*Correct all errors in the use of **irregular verbs** you may notice in your own conversation.*

Questions—What is a regular verb? An irregular verb? A defective verb? Which are the defective verbs? What are redundant verbs? Give examples.

97. ORDER OF PARSING

1. A verb, and why? 2. Regular or irregular, and why? 3. Give its principal parts. 4. Copulative, transitive, or intransitive, and why? 5. Voice, and why? 6. Mode, and why? 7. Tense, and why? 8. Person and number, and why? Rule.

98. MODELS FOR PARSING

I. "Liberty is sweet."

Is is a *verb*; it is a word which denotes being: *irregular*; it does not form its past tense and perfect participle by adding *d* or *ed* to the present indicative: *principal parts* are pres. *am*, past ind. *was*, perf. part. *been: copulative*; it asserts that the predicate describes the subject: *indicative mode*; it asserts a fact: *present tense*; it denotes present time: *third person, singular number*, to agree with its subject "liberty." Rule XIII. "A verb must agree with its subject in person and number."

II. "I shall go if you remain."

Shall go is a *verb, irregular*: give its principal parts; *intransitive*; it does not require an object to complete its meaning: *indicative mode; future tense*; it denotes future time: *first person, singular number*. Rule XIII. "A verb must agree with its subject in person and number."

Remain is a *verb, regular*; it forms its past indicative and perfect participle by adding *ed* to the present indicative: give the principal parts: *intransitive; subjunctive mode*; it represents an act as doubtful or conditional; *present tense; second person, singular or plural number*: Rule XIII.

III. "The boy caught the horse."

Caught is a *verb, irregular*; give the principal parts: *transitive*; it requires an object to complete its meaning: *active voice*; it represents its subject as acting: *indicative mode; past tense; third person, singular number*: Rule XIII.

IV. "We heard the owl hooting."

Hooting is a *participle*; it partakes of the properties of a verb and an adjective: *present participle*; it denotes continuance: it belongs to "owl." Rule XII. "An adjective or a participle belongs to some noun or pronoun."

V. "I study to improve."

To improve is a *verb*, *regular*; give the principal parts: *transitive*; *active voice*; *infinitive mode*; it expresses action without affirming it: it depends upon "study." Rule XVI. "An infinitive not used as a noun depends upon the word it limits."

99. COMPOSITION

Read the following description a number of times, then reproduce it from memory.

SUGAR

Sugar is obtained from many plants. The sweet taste of all kinds of fruit is because of the sugar in their juices. Grapes contain grape sugar, which may be seen in small white grains in raisins, or dried grapes. The sap of the maple and some other forest trees contains sugar. In France, sugar is made from beet roots in large quantities.

The sugar cane, however, contains so much sweet juice that it is cultivated in preference to all other plants for the making of sugar. It is a tall grass which grows in many hot countries. When ripe, the stems are cut down and passed between heavy rollers. The juice is thus squeezed out, and it is boiled as soon as possible. After being boiled to a syrup, the liquid is skimmed and placed in large flat pans to cool.

While cooling, a curious change takes place. Part of the syrup forms itself into small crystals. The part that will not crystallize is drained off and is called molasses. The crystallized part is called raw or moist sugar. In this state it is put into barrels and shipped to the refinery. The impurities which cause its dark color and rank taste are removed by refining.

Describe the process of tapping the **maple tree**, *gathering the* **sap**, *and making* **maple sugar**.

Analyze the following sentences, and parse the **nouns, pronouns, adjectives, verbs, and participles**.

1. Clarence has been chosen captain. 2. They might have finished their task yesterday. 3. The crops were destroyed by grasshoppers. 4. The children were playing croquet. 5. He did not return my umbrella. 6. Is he writing a letter? 7. Help us to help each other.

8. No cheating nor bargaining will ever get a single thing out of Nature's "establishment" at half price.—*Ruskin.*

9. Think that day lost whose low descending sun
    Views from thy hand no noble action done.

10. May is a pious fraud of the almanac,
    A ghastly parody of real spring,
    Shaped out of snow and breathed with eastern winds.—*Lowell.*

*Write the first two sentences of a composition entitled, "Industrious Boys."
Parse the verbs.*

Finish the composition.

100. FALSE SYNTAX

Caution I—Never use **will** for **shall**, **would** for **should**, nor **can** for **may**, as in these incorrect examples.

Ex.—1. I was afraid I would be hurt. 2. If I would try, I would learn fast. 3. I shall go; no one will prevent me. 4. I would be very careless if I left my books at home. 5. Can I have a cookie?

Caution II—**Tense forms** should express **time** in harmony with that indicated by other parts of the sentence.

Ex.—1. They have visited us yesterday. 2. You may take a walk after you finish your task. 3. He was tardy every day this week. 4. I would help you if you can't get someone else to do so. 5. He was under obligation to have assisted me.

Caution III—**General truths** should be expressed in the **present tense**.

Ex.—1. I have heard that each star was a sun. 2. I always thought that meteors were falling stars. 3. What did you say was the capital of Indiana? 4. I always thought that dew fell.

Caution IV—Do not use the **perfect participle** to express **past time**, nor the **past tense** form instead of the **perfect participle**.

Ex.—1. He come here last week. 2. I seen him when he done it. 3. The tree had fell and it was broke in two. 4. The squirrel had ran up a tree. 5. He set down on a log. 6. I have saw the man.

Caution V—**Avoid** the awkward use of **participles** in place of other forms.

Ex.—1. He neglected the plowing of his land. 2. Be ashamed of being found in bad company. 3. He likes the taking of long drives.

Caution VI—Do not use **aint** for **is not**, or **might of** for **might have**, etc.

Ex.—1. It aint one swallow that makes a summer. 2. Jane aint got her lesson done. 3. Aint you going to the concert? 4. Sam might of done his work long ago. 5. He should of taken the train.

*Correct all **inaccuracies** in the use of **verbs** you may observe in your own language.*

Correct the following sentences by reference to Rules XIII and XIV.

1. Henry and Charles was very much disappointed. 2. You was there, I suppose. 3. The yoke of oxen were sold for eight hundred dollars. 4. Ellen are not at school today. 5. The scissors is dull. 6. The fleet were seen off Hateras. 7. Time and tide waits for no man.

101. THE ADVERB—CLASSES

1. Adverbs are divided into five classes: adverbs of *time, place, cause, manner,* and *degree.*

2. **Adverbs of time** answer the questions *When? How long? How often?*

Ex.—After, again, always, early, never, frequently, hereafter, lately, immediately, now, often, seldom, then, when, etc.

3. **Adverbs of place** answer the question *Where?*

Ex.—Above, below, here, there, herein, somewhere, far, yonder, forth, away, backwards, first, etc.

4. **Adverbs of cause** answer the question *Why?*

Ex.—Therefore, then, why.

5. **Adverbs of manner** answer the question *How?*

Ex.—Amiss, anyhow, well, badly, easily, sweetly, indeed, no, perhaps, etc.

6. **Adverbs of degree** answer the questions, *How much? How little?*

Ex.—Almost, enough, even, equally, much, more, little, wholly, partly, only, scarcely, nearly, too, chiefly, etc.

7. An **adverbial phrase** is a combination of words used and parsed as a single adverb; as, *"In general," "hand in hand," "no more."*

8. **Conjunctive adverbs** are those which connect two propositions, one of which is used as an adverbial element.

Ex.—"I shall see you *when* I return." The conjunctive adverb "when" connects the two clauses, "I shall see you" and "I return." The entire second clause modifies "shall see" in the first clause, and "when" modifies "return" in the second.

102. COMPARISON OF ADVERBS

1. Many adverbs admit of comparison.

2. Three adverbs are compared by adding *er* and *est* to the simple form, viz.: *fast, faster, fastest; often, oftener, oftenest; soon, sooner, soonest.*

3. Adverbs ending in *ly* are usually compared by prefixing *more* and *most*, *less* and *least* to the simple form; as *wisely, more wisely, most wisely; swiftly, less swiftly, least swiftly.*

4. Some adverbs are compared irregularly; as, *well, better, best; little, less, least.*

Rem.—Do not confuse *good*, the adjective, with *well*, the adverb. (He plays well. He is a good player.) Both words form their comparative and superlative by *better* and *best*.

103. ORDER OF PARSING

1. An adverb, and why? 2. Compare it. 3. Tell what it modifies. Rule.

104. MODELS FOR PARSING

I. "The soldiers fought bravely."

Bravely is an *adverb*; it is used to modify the meaning of a verb: *compared*, *pos.* bravely, *com.* more bravely, *sup.* most bravely; it modifies "fought." Rule XVII. "Adverbs modify verbs, adjectives, participles, and adverbs."

II. "I will go whenever you wish."

Whenever is an *adverb*; *conjunctive*; it connects two clauses; it modifies "wish": Rule XVII.

Analyze the following sentences, and parse the nouns, pronouns, adjectives, verbs, and adverbs.

1. I saw him frequently. 2. You must call often. 3. How rapidly the moments fly. 4. He has been reproved again and again. 5. Perhaps he can tell you. 6. Doubtless, he is a wise man. 7. Peradventure, the old dragon is asleep. 8. I have not seen him since I returned from California. 9. The mystery will be explained by and by. 10. He visits us now and then.
11.   Live and love,
         Doing both nobly, because lowlily.
     Live and work, strongly, because patiently.—*Mrs. Browning.*

105. COMPOSITION

Write a description of "The Apple" using the following plan.

Plan—1. Form. 2. Parts—peel, pulp, etc. 3. Color. 4. Taste. 5. Different kinds. 6. Uses—how eaten, made into sauce, pies, etc. 7. Process of making cider. 8. Where found.

Write a description of some of these products, using the following general plan.

General Plan—1. What part of the plant growth is it? 2. Brief description of the plant. 3. Where and how is the plant raised? 4. How procured and prepared for food or manufacture? 5. How manufactured: products of manufacture? 6. In what forms and for what purposes used?

Hay	Straw	Starch	A peach	Gasoline
Flour	Paper	Vinegar	An orange	A strawberry

Write the first two sentences of a composition on "My Last Vacation," and parse the verbs and adverbs.

Questions—What is an adverb? How many classes of adverbs? What are adverbs of *time*? Of *place*? Of *cause*? Of *manner*? Of *degree*? What is an adverbial phrase? What are conjunctive adverbs? Are adverbs ever compared? How are three adverbs compared? How are adverbs ending in *ly* usually compared? How are other adverbs compared?

Repeat the order of parsing an adverb. Repeat the cautions.

106. THE PREPOSITION

1. The relations between words in a sentence are sometimes so obvious that they need no expression. This occurs when nouns denoting *time*, *distance*, *measure*, *direction*, or *value* follow verbs or adjectives; as, "He left *yesterday*," "He lives *south* of this town." Such nouns are said to be in the objective case without a governing word. (They may also be parsed as adverbs.)

2. The names of things following the passive forms of the verbs *ask*, *lend*, *teach*, *refuse*, *provide*, and some others are usually in the objective case without a governing word; as, "I was asked a *question*," "I was taught *grammar*."

3. The words of some phrases need not be separated in parsing; as, *in vain*, *on high*, *round and round*, *in general*, etc. Such combinations may be parsed as single words.

4. Sometimes two prepositions are used together, forming a *complex preposition*; as, "He came *from over* the sea."

107. ORDER OF PARSING

1. A preposition and why? 2. What relation does it show? 3. Rule.

108. MODELS FOR PARSING

"They went aboard the ship."

Aboard is a *preposition*; it shows the relation between its object and some other word: it shows the relation between "ship" and "went." Rule XVIII. "A preposition shows the relation of its object to the word upon which the latter depends."

Analyze the following sentences and parse the nouns and prepositions.

1. A lark reared her brood amid the corn. 2. They wandered in throngs down the valley. 3. Alice came from the village, through the woods, to our house. 4. We have seen the moon rising behind the eastern pines. 5. I came from beyond Richmond today. (Parse "today" in the objective case without a governing word by Rule VIII.) 6. I went to Detroit yesterday. 7. John came home last night. 8. They allowed themselves no relaxation.

9. To me the meanest flower that blows can give
Thoughts that do often lie too deep for tears.—*Wordsworth.*

10.   The locust by the wall
Stabs the noon silence with his sharp alarm.
A single haycart down the dusty road
Creaks slowly, with its driver fast asleep
On the load's top.—*Whittier.*

*Write the first two sentences of a description of a spruce, fir, or pine tree, and **parse** the prepositions.*

Finish the composition.

Questions—What is a preposition? Do the relations between objects of thought always need expression? When do they not need expression? What words are in the objective case without a governing word? What is a complex preposition? Can the words in all phrases be separated? How should such combinations be parsed?
Repeat the order of parsing a preposition.

109. THE CONJUNCTION

Conjunctions are divided into two general classes: *coordinate* and *subordinate*.

1. **Coordinate conjunctions** are those which join elements of the same rank or name.

Ex.—*And, but, or, nor, for.*

2. **Subordinate conjunctions** are those which join elements of different rank or name.

Ex.—*That, if, unless, as, because, since, though, for, after, until, when, where, there, how, although, before, provided, while,* etc.

3. **Correlative conjunctions** are coordinates or subordinates used in pairs, one referring or answering to the other.

Ex.—Both—and, as—as, so—as, so—that, either—or, neither—nor, if—then, though—yet, nevertheless, not only—but also, whether—or, or—or, nor—nor.

Rem.—Such combinations as *as if, as though, as well as, as soon as, forasmuch as, in order that, but also, but likewise, inasmuch as, not only,* etc., may be parsed as single conjunctions or conjunctive adverbs.

110. ORDER OF PARSING

1. A conjunction, and why? 2. Coordinate or subordinate, and why? 3. What does it connect? Rule.

111. MODELS FOR PARSING

I. "Ellen and Mary study algebra."

And is a *conjunction*; it connects words: *coordinate*; it connects words of the same rank or name: it connects "Ellen" and "Mary." Rule XIX. "Conjunctions connect words, phrases, members, and clauses."

II. "Neither Ellen nor Mary learned the lesson."

Neither . . . nor . . . are *conjunctions, correlative*; one refers or answers to the other: "neither" introduces the sentence, and "nor" connects "Ellen" and "Mary": Rule XIX.

III. "He will go if he is ready."

If is a *conjunction, subordinate*; it connects the main clause with a subordinate (adverb) clause: it connects the clause "he is ready" to the verb "will go," which it modifies: Rule XIX.

Analyze the following sentences and parse the **conjunctions**.

1. Cold and hunger awake not her care. 2. He came and went like a pleasant thought. 3. Wisdom is the principal thing; therefore get wisdom. 4. We cannot thrive unless we are industrious. 5. Though he slay me, yet will I trust in him. 6. He was not only proud, but vain also.

112. COMPOSITION

Read the following description three or four times, then reproduce it from memory.

IRON

Iron is a heavy, solid, incombustible metal, of a white color when pure. Its most useful property is its hardness, which is greater than that of any other metal. It can be made into steel, an alloy much stronger than iron.

Like most other metals, iron is rarely found in a pure state, being associated with oxygen, sulphur, and other substances. The mixture is called iron ore, and it varies much in quality and value. It is found in all countries and is very abundant in the United States, where valuable deposits of it are found in the neighborhood of coal.

In the manufacture of iron, the ore is first roasted. Many substances associated with the metal are driven off by this process. It is next subjected to a very great heat in a blast furnace. This process is called smelting. The metal is melted by the intense heat and is drawn off from the bottom of the furnace into channels made in sand. It is then called pig iron.

Pig iron is converted into wrought iron by being again smelted and stirred; after which, while still hot, it is hammered and rolled into bars. Wrought iron is strong and is therefore used where great strain has to be resisted.

Parse all the **conjunctions** *in three sentences of your reading lesson.*

Questions—What is a conjunction? Into how many classes are conjunctions divided? What are coordinate conjunctions? Subordinate conjunctions? Correlative conjunctions? How should *as if, not only*, etc., be parsed? Repeat the order of parsing a conjunction.

113. THE INTERJECTION

1. **Interjections** are expressions of emotion only. They are called interjections because they are *thrown in between* connected parts of discourse though generally found at the commencement of a sentence.

2. Most words when used as exclamations may be treated as interjections; as, "*What!* Are you crazy?" "*Revenge!*" cried he.

114. ORDER OF PARSING

1. An interjection and why? 2. Rule.

115. MODEL FOR PARSING

"What! Are you sure?"

What! is an *interjection*; it denotes some sudden emotion. Rule XX. "An interjection has no dependence upon other words."

Parse all the words in the following sentences.

1. Hah! It is a sight to freeze one! 2. Aha! You thought me blind, did you? 3. Ouch! How it burns! 4. Oh, ho! Caught you at it, didn't I?

5. Don't you hear? Don't you see?
   Hush! Look! In my tree
   I'm as happy as happy can be!

Questions—What is an interjection? Why is it called an interjection? Repeat the order of parsing an interjection.

116. COMPOSITION

Write a description of the metal, lead, using the following plan.

Plan—1. Properties—weight, color, etc. 2. Describe its ore. 3. Where found in our country. 4. How obtained. 5. How prepared for use. 6. Uses.

Describe some of these substances, using the following general plan.

General Plan—1. Properties—color, weight, transparency, opacity, etc. 2. Where found. 3. With what associated. 4. How obtained. 5. How prepared for use: separation of a metal from its ore, refining, alloying, etc. 6. Uses.

Tin	Zinc	Glass	Brass	Copper
Clay	Sand	Lime	Silver	Mercury

117. ELLIPSIS

1. **Ellipsis** is the omission of one or more words of a sentence. The words omitted are said to be understood.

Rem.—If required in analysis or parsing, the words omitted must be supplied.

2. All but the most important part of a sentence may be omitted.

1. **Nouns** may be omitted; as, "Ye are Christ's [*disciples*]."

2. **Pronouns** may be omitted; as, "[*you*] Come."

3. **Adjectives** may be omitted; as, "That kind of exercise may be good for you, but not [*good*] for me."

4. **Articles** may be omitted; as, "Henry has a notebook and [*a*] pencil."

5. **Participles** may be omitted; as, "This [*being*] done, we resumed our journey."

6. **Verbs** may be omitted; as, "To err is human; to forgive [*is*] divine."

7. **Adverbs** may be omitted; as, "He acted honorably, but you did not [*act honorably*]."

8. **Prepositions** may be omitted; as, "He gave [*to*] me an orange."

9. **Conjunctions** may be omitted; as, "A good, [*and*] wise, and truthful friend."

10. Entire **phrases** and **clauses** may be omitted; as, "You have more to do than you can accomplish; I, less [*to do than I can accomplish*]."

MODEL FOR ANALYSIS
"Forward!"

This is a *sentence, exclamatory.* Its subject and predicate are omitted by ellipsis. It is equivalent to "You march forward." **You** is the subject; **march**, the predicate, which is modified by **forward**, an adverb.

Questions—What is ellipsis? When are words said to be understood? What parts of a sentence may be omitted?

118. ABRIDGMENT

1. **Complex sentences** are often changed into simple ones by abridging their subordinate clauses.

Rem.—This is done by dropping the subject or changing its case, and by changing the copula or verbal predicate to an infinitive, a participial noun, or a participle.

2. A subordinate clause thus changed is called an **abridged proposition**.

Rem.—When the copula or principal verb is changed to the infinitive mode, a noun or pronoun used as subject or predicate is changed to the objective case.

Ex.—"I knew that it was he" = "I knew *it* to be *him*."

3. When the copula or principal verb is changed to a participial noun, the subject is changed to the possessive case, but a noun or pronoun used as the predicate, remains unchanged in the nominative.

Ex.—"I was not aware that it was he" = "I was not aware of *its* being *he*."

4. When the copula or principal verb is changed to a participle, the subject is put in the nominative case absolute with it.

Ex.—"The fair was not held, because the weather was unfavorable" = "The *weather* being unfavorable, the fair was not held."

MODELS FOR ANALYSIS

I. "I knew it to be him."

This is a *sentence, declarative, simple.*

I is the subject; **knew**, the predicate, which is modified by the abridged proposition **it to be him**, equivalent to *that it was he*, an objective element. "It" is modified by "to be him," an adjective element.

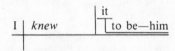

II. "I was aware of its being he."

This is a *sentence, declarative, simple.*

I is the subject; **aware**, the predicate; **was**, the copula. "Aware" is modified by the abridged proposition **of its being he**, equivalent to *that it was he*, an adverbial element. "Being" is modified by "its," an adjective element.

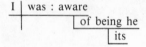

III. "The snow being deep, we could not proceed."

This is a *sentence, declarative, simple.*

We is the subject; **could proceed**, the predicate, which is modified by **not**, an adverb, and by the abridged proposition **the snow being deep**, equivalent to *because the snow was deep*, an adverbial element. "Snow" is modified by "the" and "being deep," both adjective elements.

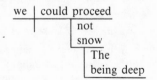

Analyze the following sentences.

1. Attention! 2. Go, Stan, go! 3. Magnificent! 4. A rope to the side! 5. Are you cold? Somewhat. 6. Better late than never. 7. I wished to be a farmer. 8. No rain having fallen, the crops were destroyed. 9. There is no danger of his falling. 10. The storm continuing, we dropped anchor. 11. Being human, he is not perfect. 12. Honor being lost, all is lost.

119. MODIFIED SUBJECT AND PREDICATE

1. The **simple**, or **grammatical subject** of a proposition is the unmodified subject.

Ex.—"A great storm is raging." "Storm" is the simple subject.

2. The **complete**, or **logical subject** is the simple subject taken with all its modifiers.

Ex.—"A great storm is raging." "A great storm" is the logical subject. "He who runs may read." "He who runs" is the complete subject.

3. The **simple** or **grammatical predicate** of a proposition is the unmodified predicate.

Ex.—"The storm rages furiously." "Rages" is the simple predicate.

4. The **complete** or **logical predicate** is the simple predicate taken with all its modifiers.

Ex.—"The storm rages furiously." "Rages furiously" is the complete predicate. "The wind blows with great violence." "Blows with great violence" is the complete predicate; "blows" is the simple predicate.

Rem.—All the parts of a sentence may be simple or complex; but it is not necessary, in analysis, to distinguish them as such. The distinction, however, may be observed with the subject and the predicate.

*Point out the **simple** and **complete** subjects and predicates in any of the preceding exercises in analysis.*

Questions—What is the simple subject of a proposition? The complete subject? The simple predicate? The complete or logical predicate?

120. COMPOSITION

Read the following description a number of times, then reproduce it from memory.

A HURRICANE IN THE WEST INDIES

A hurricane in the West Indies is generally preceded by an awe-inspiring stillness in the atmosphere. The air becomes close and heavy. The sun is red, and at night the stars seem unusually large. The mercury in the barometer falls rapidly, and the thermometer usually indicates a rise in the temperature. Darkness extends over the earth, but the upper atmosphere is lighted up by flashes of lightning.

The coming storm is first observed on the sea. Huge waves rise suddenly from its clear and motionless surface. The wind blows with unrestrained fury, and its noise may be compared to distant thunder. The rain descends in torrents; shrubs and lofty trees are borne down by the mountain streams; the rivers overflow their banks, and submerge the plains.

Terror and consternation seem to reign supreme. Land birds are driven by the wind far out to sea; sea birds seek refuge from the fury of the storm in the forests. The beasts of the field roam wildly about, or herd together trembling with fear. The elements seem to be thrown into confusion, and the stability of nature to be destroyed.

The next morning's sun shines upon a scene of utter desolation. Fertile valleys have been changed to dreary wastes. Uprooted trees, branches torn from their trunks, dead animals, and the ruins of houses have been strewed over the land. In some instances, the destruction is so complete that planters are unable to distinguish the boundaries of their estates.

Write a description of earthquakes, using the following plan.

Plan—1. Definition. 2. Cause. 3. Movements—horizontal, vertical, etc. 4. Duration of shocks. 5. Effects. 6. Where most frequent. 7. Connection with volcanic eruptions.

Describe some of these phenomena, using the following general plan.

General Plan—1. Indications of occurrence. 2. Cause. 3. Progress from beginning to end. 4. Consequences or effects of whatever character.

Mirage	A hail storm	Formation of dew
A sunset	An avalanche	A volcanic eruption
A snow storm	A thunderstorm	An eclipse of the sun

121. RULES OF SYNTAX

1. **Syntax** is that part of grammar which treats of the construction of sentences.   .

Rem.—All the exercises in the formation of sentences, in this work, are exercises in syntax.

2. A **rule of syntax** is a statement of the manner in which words should be used in sentences.

Rule I—A noun or pronoun used as the subject of a proposition is in the nominative case.

Rule II—A noun or pronoun used as the predicate of a proposition is in the nominative case.

Rule III—A noun or pronoun used to limit or modify the meaning of a noun denoting a different person or thing is in the possessive case.

Rem. 1—The modified noun is sometimes omitted; as, "We visited St. Paul's [*church*]."

Rem. 2—The modified noun need not be plural because the possessive is plural; as, "Their *intention* was good." In this case, the individuals collectively have one "intention."

Rule IV—A noun or pronoun used to limit the meaning of a noun or pronoun denoting the same person, place, or thing, is in the same case.

Rem. 1—A noun may be in apposition with a sentence, and a sentence with a noun; as, "*He is dangerously ill*—a *fact* that cannot be denied," "Remember Franklin's maxim, '*God helps them that help themselves.*'"

Rem. 2—A word in apposition with another is frequently introduced by *as*, or *or*; as, "*As mayor* of the city, *I* feel aggrieved," "mayor" being in apposition with "I"; "*Maize*, or *Indian corn*, is extensively cultivated."

Rule V—A noun or pronoun used independently is in the absolute case.

Rule VI—The object of a transitive verb in the active voice, or of its participles, is in the objective case.

Rem.—A noun or pronoun following the infinitive *to be*, is in the same case as a word which precedes it; as, "I did not think it to be *him*," "him" is in the same case as "it"; "*Whom* do you take me to be?" "whom" is in the same case as "me." See Section 118.

Rule VII—The object of a preposition is in the objective case.

Rule VIII—Nouns denoting *time, distance, measure,* or *value,* after verbs and adjectives, are in the objective case without a governing word.

Ex.—"He came home yesterday." Both "home" and "yesterday" are in the objective case without a governing word.

Rem. 1—Words denoting time, distance, measure, and direction may be parsed as adverbs instead of nouns.

Rem. 2—Nouns and pronouns following the passive forms of certain verbs, may be said to be in the objective case without a governing word; as, "I was taught *grammar;*" "He was offered a *situation.*"

Rule IX—Pronouns must agree with their antecedents in gender, person, and number.

Rem.—A pronoun used instead of a collective noun, denoting unity, should be in the neuter singular: it. One used instead of a collective noun, denoting plurality, should be plural, taking the gender of the individuals composing the collection.

Rule X—A pronoun with two or more antecedents in the singular connected by *and* must be plural.

Rem.—When the antecedents are the names of the same person or thing, the pronoun must be singular: when they are limited by *each, every,* or *no,* the pronoun must be singular: when the antecedents, taken together, are regarded as a single thing, the pronoun must be singular.

Ex.—"The *patriot* and *statesman* receives *his* reward." "Each *officer,* each *private,* did *his* duty." "*Bread and milk* was brought us, and we ate *it.*"

Rule XI—A pronoun with two or more antecedents in the singular, connected by *or* or *nor,* must be singular.

Rem.—When one of the antecedents is plural, it should be placed last, and the pronoun should be plural; as, "Neither the farmer nor his sons were aware of *their* danger."

Rule XII—An adjective or participle belongs to some noun or pronoun.

Rem.—An adjective used as a predicate belongs to the subject.

Rule XIII—A verb must agree with its subject in person and number.

Rule XIV—A verb, with two or more subjects in the singular connected by *and,* must be plural.

Rem.—When two or more subjects in the singular are but different names for the same thing, the verb should be singular; as, "Courage and valor is a mark of a good soldier." When two or more singular subjects are emphatically distinguished, the verb should be singular; as, "Every bird and every beast *cowers* before the wild blast."

Rule XV—A verb, with two or more subjects in the singular connected by *or* or *nor*, must be singular.

Rule XVI—An infinitive not used as a noun depends upon the word it limits.

Rule XVII—Adverbs modify verbs, adjectives, participles, and adverbs.

Rem.—Adverbs also modify phrases and entire propositions; as, "He lives *just* around the corner," "*Certainly*, yours is a good school."

Rule XVIII—A preposition shows the relation of its object to the word upon which the object depends.

Rule XIX—Conjunctions connect words, phrases, clauses, and members.

Rule XX—Interjections have no dependence upon other words.

122. LETTER WRITING

Letters are classified as *friendly* letters or *business* letters. A sample of each type is shown on the following pages. A sample envelope form is also shown. The envelope form is the same for both friendly letters and business letters.

Write a letter of your own, carefully following one of the samples.

Ex. 1—Sample form for addressing envelopes.

Ex. 2—Sample friendly letter.

(Heading) ——

37 Knob Hill Road
Albion, Maine 04901
April 19, 1986

Dear Sally, —— (Salutation)

    Spring is finally here in Maine, though the calendar says it arrived a month ago. The ice is gone from the river and the pussy willows are in bloom. I suppose you are still skiing in the Colorado mountains, though.

    When can you and Aunt Gladys visit New England and see us again? If you can come this summer, Mom says she wants you folks to join us at a lobster cookout on the beach.

(Body) ——

(Closing) —— Sincerely yours,
(Signature) —— Marcie

Ex. 3—Sample business letter.

Bethel Christian School
648 Oak Street
Middlebury, Michigan 49000
March 15, 1986 ——————— (Heading)

Mayor Edward Barnes
City Hall
Middlebury, Michigan 49000 ——————(Inside Address)

Dear Mayor Barnes: ———————————(Salutation)

The sixth, seventh, and eighth graders of Bethel
Christian School are celebrating our nation's
freedoms with a patriotic presentation in the
school gymnasium at 7:00 p.m. on April 19.
As you know, this is the day the Revolutionary
War began with the Battle of Bunker Hill right
after Paul Revere's famous ride. Several states
still celebrate this annually as Patriot's Day. (Body)

We would like you and Mrs. Barnes to be our
guests of honor on this day commemorating
our nation's heritage. Can we count on your
being there?

Yours truly, ———————————————(Closing)

Michael R. Jones ——————(Signature)

Michael R. Jones
President, Eighth Grade Class ——————(Name & title)

123. MISCELLANEOUS EXERCISES

1. She saw a glory in each cloud. 2. Still waters are commonly deepest. 3. Tomorrow may be brighter than today. 4. Few days pass without some clouds. 5. She made acquaintance with the birds that fluttered by. 6. It was a harper, wandering with his harp.

7. How long didst thou think that his silence was slumber? 8. At length the sun departed, setting in a sea of gold. 9. The smooth sea, the serene atmosphere, the mild zephyr, are the proper emblems of a gentle temper and a peaceful life.

10. The earth is the Lord's and the fulness thereof;
The world and they that dwell therein.—*Bible*.

11. The night, methinks, is but the daylight sick. 12. Evils have been more painful to us in the prospect than in the actual pressure. 13. A written or printed paper, posted in a public place, is called a placard. 14. Few are qualified to shine in company; but it is in most men's power to be agreeable.

15. How often have I blessed the coming day.
When toil remitting lent its turn to play,
And all the village train, from labor free,
Led up their sports beneath the spreading tree.—*Goldsmith*.

16. Alas, we think not that we daily see
About our hearths, angels that are to be,
Or may be if they will.—*Leigh Hunt*.

17. The insect tribe are here: the ant toils on
With its white burden; in its netted web
Gray glistening o'er the bush, the spider lurks,
A close-crouched ball, out-darting as a hum
Tells its trapped prey, and looping quick its threads,
Chains into helplessness the buzzing wings.—*Street*.

18. Princes have but their titles for their glories;
An outward honor for an inward toil.—*Shakespeare*.

19.   My soul is an enchanted boat
Which, like a sleeping swan, doth float
Upon the silver waves of thy sweet singing;
And thine doth like an angel sit
Beside the helm conducting it,
While all the winds with melody are ringing.—*Shelley*.

20. The year leads round the seasons in a choir
Forever charming and forever new,
Blending the grand, the beautiful, the gay,
The mournful and the tender in one strain.—*Percival*.

21. King David's limbs were weary. He had fled
    From far Jerusalem; and now he stood,
    With his faint people, for a little rest
    Upon the shores of Jordan. The light wind
    Of morn was stirring, and he bared his brow
    To its refreshing breath; for he had worn
    The mourner's covering, and he had not felt
    That he could see his people until now.—*Willis.*

22. One hour beheld him since the tide he stemmed,
    Disguised, discovered, conquering, ta'en, condemned;
    A chief on land, an outlaw on the deep,
    Destroying, saving, prisoned, and asleep.—*Byron.*

23. The heavens declare the glory of God;
    And the firmament sheweth his handywork.
    Day unto day uttereth speech,
    And night unto night sheweth knowledge.—*Bible.*

24. He that attends to his interior self,
    That has a heart, and keeps it; has a mind
    That hungers, and supplies it; and who seeks
    A social, not a dissipated life,
    Has business.—*Cowper.*

25. The timid it concerns to ask their way,
    And fear what foe in caves and swamps may stay;
    To make no step until the event is known,
    And ills to come, as evils past, bemoan.
    Not so the wise; no coward watch he keeps,
    To spy what danger on his pathway creeps.
    Go where he will, the wise man is at home—
    His hearth the earth, his hall the azure dome.—*Emerson.*

26. Every worm beneath the moon
    Draws different threads, and late or soon
    Spins toiling out his own cocoon.—*Tennyson.*

27. Sweet is the breath of morn, her rising sweet,
    With charm of earliest birds; pleasant the sun,
    When first on this delightful land he spreads
    His orient beams, on herb, tree, fruit, and flower,
    Glistening with dew.—*Milton.*

28. The day hath gone to God,—
    Straight—like an infant's spirit, or a mocked
    And mourning messenger of grace to man.—*Bailey.*

29. It is a little thing to speak a phrase
    Of common comfort, which, by daily use,
    Has almost lost its sense; yet on the ear
    Of him who thought to die unmourned, 'twill fall
    Like choicest music.—*Talfourd*.

30. A song to the oak, the brave old oak,
    Who hath ruled in the greenwood long;
    Here's health and renown to his broad green crown,
    And his fifty arms so strong.—*Chorley*.

31. Labor is life! 'Tis the still water faileth;
    Idleness ever despaireth, bewaileth;
    Keep the watch wound, for the dark rust assaileth;
    Flowers droop and die in the stillness of noon.—

    Francis S. Osgood.

PART III

PUNCTUATION

124. DEFINITION

1. **Punctuation** is the art of dividing written discourse into sentences and parts of sentences, by means of points and marks.

2. The principal marks used in punctuation are the following:

Comma . . . . ,	Exclamation point . !
Semicolon . . . . ;	Dash . . . . —
Colon . . . . :	Parentheses . . . . . ( )
Period	Brackets . . . . [ ]
Question mark . . . . ?	

125. THE COMMA

The **comma** denotes the slightest degree of separation between the parts of a sentence.

Rule I—Three or more nouns, pronouns, adjectives, verbs, or adverbs, in the same construction, should be separated by commas.

Ex.—1. Spring, summer, autumn, and winter are called the seasons. 2. You, he, and I played together. 3. David was a brave, wise, and pious man. 4. In a letter, we may advise, exhort, comfort, request, and discuss. 5. Success depends upon our acting prudently, steadily, and vigorously.

Rule II—The members of a compound sentence, when long and connected by conjunctions, should be separated by commas.

Ex.—He was not fond of the technical language of metaphysics, but he had grappled, like the giant he was, with its most formidable problems.
—Everett.

Rem.—Short compound sentences need no comma: He sang and she played.

Rule III—Two correlative clauses should be separated by commas.

Ex.—As in Adam all die, so in Christ shall all be made alive.

Rule IV—Each couplet of words arranged in pairs should be set off by commas.

Ex.—Sink or swim, live or die, I give my hand and my heart to this vote.

Rule V—Words placed in opposition to each other should be separated by commas.

Ex.—Though deep, yet clear; though gentle, yet not dull.

Rem.—This rule applies, also, to phrases and clauses placed in opposition or antithesis to each other.

Rule VI—When a verb is omitted, its place is usually supplied by a comma.

Ex.—War is the law of violence; peace, the law of love.

Rule VII—Transposed words, phrases, and clauses are usually set off by commas.

Ex.—1. Integrity is, no doubt, the first requisite. 2. Whom ye ignorantly worship, Him declare I unto you. (In "natural" order no comma is needed: I declare unto you Him whom ye ignorantly worship.)

Rule VIII—Adverbs used independently, or modifying an entire proposition should be set off by commas.

Ex.—Indeed, you must wait awhile.

Rule IX—Nouns and pronouns in the nominative absolute case by pleonasm or direct address, should be separated from the rest of the sentence by commas.

Ex.—1. Our souls, how heavily they go to reach immortal joys. 2. Take, O boatman, thrice thy fee!

Rule X—Nouns in apposition modified by other words than *the*, should be set off by commas.

Ex.—The butterfly, child of the summer, flutters in the sun.

Rem.—Nouns in apposition introduced by *or* or *as*, should be set off by commas.

Rule XI—A direct quotation should be set off by commas.

Ex.—Quoth the raven, "Nevermore."

Rule XII—Words repeated for emphasis should be set off by commas.

Ex.—Verily, verily, I say unto you.

126. THE SEMICOLON

The **semicolon** denotes a degree of separation greater than that denoted by the comma.

Rule I—The semicolon should be used before *as*, *namely*, etc., introducing an example or an illustration.

Ex.—There are four seasons; namely, spring, summer, autumn, and winter.

Rule II—The semicolon is used between clauses of compound sentences joined by conjunctions as *therefore*, *however*, *nevertheless*, *accordingly*, *thus*, *then*, or *hence*.

Ex.—We went to the fair; however we did not get to see the ox pull.

Rem.—A semicolon is not needed with the conjunctions *and*, *but*, or *or*.

Ex.—We went to the fair but we missed the ox pull.

Rule III—Semicolons should separate the clauses of compound sentences if the connective is omitted, if their parts are separated by commas, or if the clauses are long.

Ex.—1. Straws swim upon the surface; pearls lie at the bottom. 2. Philosophers say that God's creation is unlimited in its operations; that it has inexhaustible treasures in reserve; that knowledge will always be progressive; and that all future generations will continue to make discoveries, of which we have not the least idea.

127. THE COLON

The **colon** denotes a degree of separation greater than that indicated by the semicolon.

Rule I—The colon should precede an example, a list, or a lengthy quotation, and it should follow the introduction to a speech.

Ex.—The Scriptures give us a pleasant description of our Creator in these words: "God is love."

Rule II—The colon is used with certain numeral combinations: to separate hours from minutes, as 6:30 p.m.; to separate Bible chapters from verses, as John 3:16; and to separate a volume and a page number, as *Harpers* 203:37.

128. THE PERIOD

The **period** denotes the greatest degree of separation.

Rule I—The period should be placed at the end of a declarative or an imperative sentence.

Ex.—1. Evil companions corrupt good morals. 2. Walk quietly.

Rule II—The period should be used after every abbreviated word.

Ex.—H. G. Lloyd, Jr.; Mich., Ind., Ill.; Ps. 75:4-7; Chap. XIV.

129. QUESTION MARK

The question mark denotes that a question is asked.

Ex.—1. Where is Singapore? 2. Do you own this farm?

130. EXCLAMATION POINT

The **exclamation point** denotes passion or emotion.

Rule I—The exclamation point should be placed after expressions denoting strong emotion.

Ex.—1. Alas, poor Yorick! 2. Fie on you! 3. Ouch!

131. THE DASH

The **dash** is a straight, horizontal line placed between the parts of a sentence.

Rule I—The dash should be used where a sentence breaks off abruptly, or where there is a change in its meaning or construction.

Ex.—1. Dim—dim—I faint—darkness comes over me. 2. How he wished that he could see his friend once more—how earnestly he wished it.

Rule II—The dash is frequently used before and after a parenthesis—the marks of parenthesis being omitted.

Ex.—They see three of the cardinal virtues of dog or man—courage, endurance, and skill—in intense action.

Rem.—The dash is frequently used where there is an omission of letters or figures; as, Luke 1—4 to indicate chapters 1, 2, 3, and 4 of Luke.

132. THE MARKS OF PARENTHESIS

The **marks of parenthesis** enclose an expression which has no necessary connection, in sense or construction, with the sentence in which it is inserted.

Rem.—Such an expression is called a *parenthesis*.

Rule I—The parentheses should include only words which may be omitted without changing the meaning of the sentence.

Ex.—1. My gun was on my arm (as it always is in that district), but I let the weasel kill the rabbit.

2. Know, then, this truth (enough for man to know),
Virtue alone is happiness below.—*Pope.*

Rem.—The parentheses sometimes include letters or figures used to enumerate subjects or divisions of a subject; as, "(*a*) What it does; (*b*) What it is."

133. THE BRACKETS

Brackets are used to include words, phrases, or clauses explaining what precedes them, or correcting an error.

Ex.—1. They [the Indians] are fast disappearing. 2. I differ with [from] you in opinion.

134. OTHER MARKS USED IN WRITING

I. The **apostrophe** ['] is used to denote the omission of one or more letters, or to mark the possessive case; as, "You're mistaken," "The Queen's English."

II. The **hyphen** [-] is used (1) to join the parts of compound words and expressions; as, "Nut-brown maid;" (2) to divide words into syllables; as, "con-fu-sion;" (3) after a syllable at the end of a line, when the rest of the word is carried to the next line.

III. **Quotation marks** [" "] are used to show that a passage is taken *verbatim* from some author; as, Shakespeare says, "All the world's a stage."

IV. The **asterisk** [*] refers to notes in the margin, or at the bottom of the page.

V. The **brace** [⏜] connects a number of words with a common term.

VI. The **tilde** [ñ] annexes to *n* the sound of *y*; as, cañon, pronounced *canyon*: the **cedilla** [ç] gives to *c* the sound of *s*; as, façade.

VII. The **acute accent** ['] commonly denotes a sharp sound: the **grave accent** ['] a depressed sound.

Rem.—In most reading books, the *acute* accent denotes the rising inflection; the *grave* accent, the falling inflection.

Suggestion to Teachers—Require pupils to give rules for the use of all the points found in their reading lesson. Select passages from good authors and pronounce the words in consecutive order, as in a spelling lesson, without indicating the grammatical construction by tone of voice or inflections. Let the pupils write these as pronounced, and separate them into sentences and parts of sentences by the proper points.

Punctuate properly the following example and observe the rules for the use of capitals.

his personal appearance contributed to the attraction of his social intercourse his countenance frame expression and presence arrested and fixed attention you could not pass him unnoticed in a crowd nor fail to observe in him a man of high mark and character no one could see him and not wish to see more of him and this alike in public and private.

edward everett,

jack was a clever boy strong goodnatured and ready with his hands but he did not go out to work for a living staying at home instead and helping his mother about the house and garden he chopped wood to make the fire dug and weeded the little vegetable patch and milked their one cow milky white the widow cooked and cleaned and mended so that the two of them though they were poor lived in contentment and had enough to eat and drink

jack said his mother one day when they had not had enough rain to grow grass for milky white dont you think wed better sell her we must have money for food and drink

Questions—What is punctuation? Define the principal marks used in punctuation. Repeat the rules for their use.

What does the apostrophe denote? For what purposes is the hyphen used? The quotation marks? The asterisk? What does the brace connect?

What does the tilde denote? The cedilla? What does the acute accent denote? The grave accent? What do these denote in most reading books?

APPENDIX

IRREGULAR VERBS

The following list contains the **principal parts** of most of the irregular verbs. Those marked R have also the regular forms.

PRESENT	PAST	PERFECT PARTICIPLE	PRESENT	PAST	PERFECT PARTICIPLE
Abide	abode	abode	Cleave	cleft	cleft, R
Am	was	been	(split)	clove	cloven
Arise	arose	arisen			cleaved
Awake	awoke, R	awoke, R	Cling	clung	clung
Bear	bore	born	Clothe	clad, R	clad, R
(bring forth)			Come	came	come
Bear (carry)	bore	borne	Cost	cost	cost
Beat	beat	beaten	Creep	crept	crept
		beat	Crow	crew, R	crowed
Become	became	become	Cut	cut	cut
Befall	befell	befallen	Deal	dealt	dealt
Beget	begat	begotten	Dig	dug, R	dug, R
	begot	begot	Do	did	done
Begin	began	begun	Draw	drew	drawn
Behold	beheld	beheld	Dream	dreamt, R	dreamt, R
Bend	bent, R	bent, R	Drive	drove	driven
Bereave	bereft, R	bereft, R	Dwell	dwell, R	dwelt
Beseech	besought	besought	Eat	ate	eaten
Bet	bet	bet	Fall	fell	fallen
Bid	bid	bid	Feed	fed	fed
		bidden	Feel	felt	felt
Bind	bound	bound	Fight	fought	fought
Bite	bit	bitten	Find	found	found
		bit	Flee	fled	fled
Bleed	bled	bled	Fling	flung	flung
Bless	blest, R	blest, R	Fly	flew	flown
Break	broke	broken	Forbear	forbore	forborne
		broke	Forget	forgot	forgotten
Breed	bred	bred			forgot
Bring	brought	brought	Forsake	forsook	forsaken
Build	built, R	built, R	Freeze	froze	frozen
Burst	burst	burst	Freight	freighted	fraught, R
Buy	bought	bought	Get	got	got
Cast	cast	cast			gotten
Catch	caught	caught	Give	gave	given
Choose	chose	chosen	Go	went	gone
Cleave	cleaved	cleaved	Grave	graven, R	graven, R
(adhere)			Grind	ground	ground

PRESENT	PAST	PERFECT PARTICIPLE	PRESENT	PAST	PERFECT PARTICIPLE
Grow	grew	grown	Set	set	set
Hang	hung	hung	Shake	shook	shaken
(R. when it means *to execute*)			Shear	shorn, R	shorn, R
Have	had	had	Shed	shed	shed
Hear	heard	heard	Shine	shone, R	shone, R
Hew	hewed	hewn, R	Shoe	shod	shod
Hide	hid	hidden	Shoot	shot	shot
		hid	Show	showed	shown
Hit	hit	hit	Shred	shred, R	shred
Hold	held	held	Shrink	shrunk	shrunk
Hurt	hurt	hurt		shrank	shrunken
Keep	kept	kept	Shut	shut	shut
Kneel	knelt, R	knelt	Sing	sang	sung
Knit	knit, R	knit, R		sung	
Know	knew	known	Sink	sank	sunk
Lay	laid	laid		sunk	
Lead	led	led	Sit	sat	sat
Lean	leant, R	leant, R	Slay	slew	slain
Leap	leapt, R	leapt, R	Sleep	slept	slept
Learn	learnt, R	learnt, R	Sling	slung	slung
Leave	left	left	Slink	slunk	slunk
Lend	lent	lent	Slit	slit	slit
Let	let	let	Smite	smote	smitten
Lie (recline)	lay	lain			smote
Light	lit, R	lit, R	Sow (scatter)	sowed	sown, R
Load	loaded	laden, R	Speak	spoke	spoken
Lose	lost	lost	Speed	sped	sped, R
Make	made	made	Spend	spent	spent
Mean	meant	meant	Spin	spun	spun
Meet	met	met	Spit	spit	spit
Mow	mowed	mown, R	(R. when it means *to impale*)		
Pass	past, R	past		spat	
Pay	paid	paid	Split	split	split
Plead	plead, R	plead, R	Spoil	spoilt, R	spoilt, R
	pled	pled	Spread	spread	spread
Put	put	put	Spring	sprang	sprung
Quit	quit, R	quit, R		sprung	
Read	read	read	Stand	stood	stood
Rend	rent	rent	Steal	stole	stolen
Rid	rid	rid	Stick	stuck	stuck
Ride	rode	ridden	Sting	stung	stung
		rode	Stride	strode	stridden
Ring	rang	rung	Strike	struck	struck
	rung				stricken
Rise	rose	risen	String	strung	strung
Rive	riven, R	riven, R	Strive	strove	striven, R
Run	ran	run	Sweep	swept	swept
Saw	sawed	sawn, R	Swell	swelled	swollen, R
Say	said	said	Swim	swam	swum
See	saw	seen		swum	
Seek	sought	sought	Swing	swung	swung

PRESENT	PAST	PERFECT PARTICIPLE	PRESENT	PAST	PERFECT PARTICIPLE
Take	took	taken	Wear	wore	worn
Teach	taught	taught	Weave	wove, R	woven, R
Tear	tore	torn	Weep	wept	wept
Tell	told	told	Wed	wed, R	wed, R
Think	thought	thought	Wet	wet, R	wet, R
Thrive	throve, R	thriven, R	Whet	whet, R	whet, R
Throw	threw	thrown	Win	won	won
Thrust	thrust	thrust	Wind	wound	wound
Tread	trod	trodden	Work	wrought, R	wrought, R
		trod	Wring	wrung	wrung
Wake	woke, R	woke, R	Write	wrote	written

UNIPERSONAL VERBS

A **unipersonal verb** is one by which an act or state is asserted independently of any particular subject; as, "It snows;" "It behooves us to be watchful." In each of these sentences, "it" represents an indefinite subject. The term "unipersonal" need not be used in parsing.

CAPITAL LETTERS, ITALICS, ETC.

I. The first word of every sentence should begin with a capital letter.

II. The first word of every line of poetry should begin with a capital letter.

III. Proper names of persons, places, days, etc., should begin with capital letters.

IV. Titles of honor or distinction should begin with capital letters.

V. All appellations of the Deity should begin with capital letters.

VI. Words denoting nationality should begin with capital letters.

VII. Most words derived from proper names should begin with capital letters.

VIII. Words of special importance may begin with capital letters.

IX. I and O, used as single words, should be capitals.

X. Emphatic words, phrases, and clauses are frequently printed in capitals.

Rem.—Italicized words in the King James Bible are those supplied by translators to explain the original.